MOVEMENT AND REVOLUTION

Peter L. Berger, Professor of Sociology at the New School for Social Research and editor of its quarterly, *Social Research,* is author of, among other books, *Invitation to Sociology, A Rumor of Angels, The Sacred Canopy* and co-author of *The Social Construction of Reality.*

Richard J. Neuhaus, senior pastor of the Lutheran Church of St. John the Evangelist in the Williamsburg/Bedford-Stuyvesant section of Brooklyn, is editor of *Una Sancta,* a journal of theology, a member of the Coalition for a Democratic Alternative (CDA), and on the Board of Directors of SANE. In 1968 he was a delegate to the Democratic National Convention in Chicago, where he was arrested in a protest against the denial of civil liberties.
Both authors have been active in Clergy and Laymen Concerned About Vietnam, and this book grew out of their common concern about American involvement in Vietnam and related issues.

MOVEMENT
AND REVOLUTION

PETER L. BERGER

AND RICHARD JOHN NEUHAUS

ANCHOR BOOKS
Doubleday & Company, Inc./Garden City, New York

To Brigitte

wife to one,
friend to the other,
adamant critic of both

First Anchor edition published simultaneously
with hardcover, 1970 by Doubleday & Company, Inc.

Anchor Books edition: 1970

CONTENTS

CONTENTS

PREFACE

The conversation of which this book is part began with theology rather than politics. Indeed, the first time we met we talked about the conflict between the death of children and the justice of God. We see in retrospect a striking continuity between that first talk and the subject at hand. In the following pages we return again and again to the relation of compassion to justice. To be sure, this is not a theological book, yet in our own minds the subject of movement and revolution touches upon the most fundamental questions about the human condition. We shall not develop our theological concerns here, but the reader ought to know where this conversation began.

Over the last several years we have not only talked about political questions, but have had occasion to work on them together. During this time we discovered basic differences in our political perspectives. We also discovered significant areas of agreement. The differences are those usually characterized as those distinguishing radical from conservative. We share what we hope is the reader's skepticism about the adequacy of these labels. They are, however, as inescapable as they are inadequate. We had best say what we mean by radical and conservative.

The distinction between radical and conservative rests upon different views of politics and history. The radical believes politics to be more crucially significant for the realization of man. For him, a larger sphere of human life must be "politicized." The conservative, on the other hand, is supicious of the political enterprise itself. The slogans and programs of political change seem to him more threat than promise. As for history, the radical gives greater credence to the idea of the genuinely new. An "age of discontinuity" is welcomed as an age of new possibilities. The conservative, on the other hand, is inclined to anticipate the future as more of the same. Behind discontinuity he perceives the threat of chaos. Obviously these differences are relative, but they can become relevant to the manner in which specific problems are approached, as these essays will show.

Our hope that people with significantly different political perspectives can work together has emerged from agreement and co-operation on real issues, not simply from theoretical speculation. Notable among these have been Vietnam, American policies in the Third World, and the racial crisis. We have both been outraged by the atrocious actions of the United States in Vietnam and have worked together in opposition to that war. Our view of the relationship between American power and the Third World was sharpened during the very weeks when we were planning this book in Mexico. We see the racial crisis from different vantage points, one of us living in a white-liberal enclave, the other deeply immersed in the black community itself. Both locations are in Brooklyn, and, while we are not insensitive to the influence of our respective zip codes on our political views, both of us are personally involved with the struggle to humanize urban America. We have felt and been rewarded by our divergencies in basic political outlook, but are also impressed by our remarkable agreement on specified analyses and actions. We know that, pushed far enough, our differences could put us on opposite sides of the barricades. But we are persuaded that there is much to talk about and to do together before that issue must be joined.

We do not regard ourselves as so important that our conversation will be of intrinsic interest to others. It is precisely because our understandings emerge from conversation about issues that are not unique to us but grip millions of thoughtful Americans that we hope this book will be useful to others.

P . L . B .
R . J . N .

Brooklyn, N.Y.
St. Matthew 1969

BETWEEN SYSTEM AND HORDE

Personal Suggestions to Reluctant Activists

PETER L. BERGER

1. On Political Activity

The only political commitments worth making are those that seek to reduce the amount of human suffering in the world. Much of politics, of course, is too ordinary to evoke commitment of any depth. Most of the rest is crime, illusion, or the self-indulgence of intellectuals.

Politics is the process by which power is acquired and exercised in human affairs. There can be no society, or indeed no human group of even moderate size and continuity, without this process. Thus there will always be individuals who act in society as men of politics, be it professionally or as amateurs. It is quite possible to do this, even to do it with considerable seriousness, without making politics an object of profound personal commitment. In other words, politics can be a task, a game, or even a vocation for some individuals, without absorbing them as persons and also without presenting itself to others as a moral imperative. Politics carried on in this attitude can be good, bad, or indifferent, but it is unlikely to produce the violent social upheavals that are the common results of politics raised to the dignity of intense commitment. Today, in America and elsewhere, we are constantly assailed by the assertion that intense political commitment is always good and that it is mandatory for everyone. It is, therefore, important to begin by challenging both these propositions.

Intense political commitment is usually bad. It is bad in its motives. It is bad in its consequences. As to consequences, it is very difficult to look at history and con-

14   *Peter L. Berger*

clude that most of the great upheavals produced by the
politically committed could not have been avoided, to the
great advantage of the people living during and after the
period in which these upheavals actually took place. We
shall return to this point later when we discuss the
question of revolution. As to motives, the historical parade
of the great committed ones is hardly an inspiring spectacle. The motives that predominate are rooted in crime,
fanaticism, and personal pathology, or in some combination
of these. To some, politics is the arena in which to
indulge their overwhelming lust for domination. To some,
politics is the sphere of faith and redemption, imbued
in consequence with the peculiar intolerance of (typically
frustrated) religious hopes. To others, political commitment is a way of escaping from their own inner turmoil—
for them, politics *must* be full of upheavals, since only a
maximum of social violence can assuage the violence
raging within themselves (by, so to speak, "equalizing the
pressure"). Most of this is morally repulsive. It becomes
especially repulsive when these motives are cloaked in
the ideological rhetoric at which intellectuals are adept.
In all likelihood intellectuals are no more prone than
others to criminal ambition, frustrated faith, and minds
haunted by chaos. They are only so much better at
convincing themselves and their audiences that they are
really moved by quite different things.

But there is one other motive for intense political
commitment that is of a different moral order. That is
the motive of compassion. It is possible to be moved
to political commitment—*not* by wanting power, *not* by
seeking some sort of religious fulfillment, *not* because
one needs it psychologically—but because one chooses to
involve oneself in the plight of one's fellow men. It is
this motive, and this motive only, that I propose to treat
with moral respect. Indeed, it is to individuals with this
motive that the present essay is addressed. The others,
I have found, I'm not very good at talking to anyway.

Now, it is clear that not every instance of compassion

leads logically to political commitment. Human beings suffer for many reasons and much of this suffering is not amenable to mitigation by political means. One of the severe shortcomings of contemporary "pan-politicalism" is a failure to understand this—a failure that is finally due to a (probably deliberate) avoidance of the reality of human finitude and mortality. All the same, a large amount of human suffering is in fact caused by the social arrangements under which men live, and is thus, at least in principle, amenable to political treatment by virtue of the changes that the exercise of power can bring about in these arrangements. Very probably this "political sector" of human suffering has increased substantially in our own time, because the complexity of life under modern conditions has augmented the importance of all the arrangements we now call "society." In other words, probably more people today suffer not just from the human condition in general but from very specific social arrangements, and conversely more human suffering is open to attack by the instruments of political activity.

Let us return to the motive of compassion, though. It implies a participation in the suffering of *others*. This, I think, is very important. Individuals can, of course, be moved to political activity of one kind or another by virtue of suffering *themselves*. But such activity cannot as yet be called a commitment in any morally significant way, unless it entails solidarity with others who are suffering. Political commitment without human solidarity is typically a form of crime, more or less morally abhorrent as circumstances dictate. Albert Camus, in *The Rebel*, has given us a classic discussion of this essential difference between the solitary "I" and the collective "we" in the morality of rebellion—a moral differentiation that is, I think, applicable to political activity generally, beyond the narrower area of rebellion. Political commitment arising from compassion is thus, minimally, rooted in solidarity with those others who are suffering in the same place or in the same way as oneself. Political commitment may also arise, however, from compassion with others whose circumstances are quite different from one's own. It is this latter kind that is one of the most hopeful phenomena on the American scene today.

Political commitment is *not* always good. It may be good, at least in its motives (not necessarily therefore also in its consequences), if it arises out of compassion with human suffering. Moreover, political commitment is *not* a universal imperative. One of the several totalitarian features of contemporary "pan-politicalism" is its insistence that politics, at all times and in all places, ought to be the concern of everyone. This great lapse of the imagination is one of the most dubious blessings of modern democracy. It has reached a grotesque climax in the "participatory" ideal of the contemporary left. It is of fundamental importance to reiterate, in the face of these ideological aberrations, that human life is infinitely richer in its possibilities of fulfillment than in its political expressions, and that it is indeed a basic human right to live apolitically—a right that may be denied only for the most urgent reasons. For most of human history, politics has been left to the few whose vocation it was supposed to be, leaving the many to go about their own (possibly much more interesting) business. In other words, "we" lived our lives, while "they" took care of political matters. I'm not at all persuaded by the democratic dogma that the *necessary* result of this division of labor is tyranny and exploitation; actually, a pretty good case could be made for the contrary proposition. Be this as it may, there is nothing intrinsically wicked about leaving politics to "them." It all depends on what "they" are doing—and, needless to say, on what "we" propose to do instead. Recently, it seems to me, "they" have done such a bad job that "we," even we who have no political inclinations whatever, could hardly have done any worse. This, of course, is in a nutshell the story of the "politicalization" of many Americans in the last few years. But it is one thing to be "politicized" in a particular situation, quite another to make a *Weltanschauung* out of this.

My first suggestion, then, is that one be unashamedly niggardly in one's political engagements. My second suggestion is that, having been forced out of a reluctance to engage in politics by solidarity with other men, one make every effort to remember that life consists of more than politics. As far as my own *Weltanschauung* is concerned, the first suggestion is related to the conviction that there is a rightful way of life that is called contemplation; the second suggestion, to the conviction that there is no activity, however important, that should be allowed to supersede the capacity for laughter. This having been admitted, it will not be hard to see why I find most political activists thoroughly uncongenial—and those who deem themselves revolutionaries most of all. Activists by inclination, almost to a man, are contemptuous of contemplation and just about irremediably humorless. Activists by force of circumstance (that is, people like "us," who'd much rather do something else than politics) must remain very vigilant so as not to be drawn into the frenetic and grim world of the "politicals."

Implied in the foregoing, of course, is the view that our situation in America is one that calls for political activity, however little one may welcome or enjoy this. There is nothing at all original in the evidences that have brought me to this conclusion. These have been, above all else, the continuing deprivation of racial minorities in America and the unjust American war in Vietnam. Both of these facts, as personal touchstones and as objective symptoms, have made evident to me, as to very many others, that there is indeed something "radically wrong" about America —the wrongness put in glaring perspective by the unparalleled economic and technological power of America, as well as by the grandiloquent promise of American political ideals. Nor can there by any doubt, however one may analyze just what it is that is wrong (and on this my own analyses differ sharply from those of many others who have been similarly aroused), that the suffering we confront in these facts is, in principle, within the political sphere. It is not the human condition that afflicts American Negroes and the Vietnamese today. It is rather very specific American social arrangements and government policies. And it is within the capacity of political power to change such arrangements and policies. The "politicalization" of large numbers of Americans in recent years thus requires neither a moral excuse nor an ideological justification. It has been grounded in what is both the most praiseworthy and the most enduring motive for political commitment—participation in the agony of one's time.

For humanly responsive Americans, then, this is a time for political activity. To say this, of course, is not to prejudge what particular political course one will embark on or in what attitude one will engage in political activity. I shall discuss these questions through the rest of this essay. But these opening considerations already suggest a very broad but nonetheless useful guideline for political engagements. To wit, they suggest a criterion for moral credibility in politics. Those who commit themselves to political action out of compassion for and solidarity with human suffering have certain traits in common. They put human beings ahead of principles, doctrines, or grand designs. They seek to avoid the infliction of pain—not only in some Utopian future, but here and now. They are painstakingly miserly in calculating the human costs of their political programs. And when these costs, out of real or imagined necessity, are high, they are afflicted by an overpowering anguish—an anguish from which they do not run away, and of which they are not ashamed. Because of all this, they are prone to the particular moderation that comes from reason—not the doctrinaire reason of the ideologist, but the pragmatic reason of the man who seeks to attain his goals at the least possible human cost. Indeed, the criterion suggested here resolves itself into a combination of compassion *and* reason. The observance of this criterion will protect one from the ineffectiveness of compassion without reason—and from the inhumanity of reason without compassion—both political constellations that are not exactly scarce these days.

First suggested maxim for political activity: *Only believe those whose motives are compassionate and whose programs stand the test of rational inquiry.*

Second suggested maxim for political activity: *When it comes to revolutionaries, only trust the sad ones. The enthusiastic ones are the oppressors of tomorrow—or else they are only kidding.*

Unrealistic maxims? I don't think so. One must learn to listen to people—not just to what they say but to how they say it. The criminals, the fanatics, and the psychopaths, of course, can use the language of compassion in their political rhetoric. But it is their voices that betray them. The thirst for domination, the intoxication with a "redeeming" system, the dark thrust of madness—these are motives that are hard to control over a period of time. One must, therefore, listen carefully and patiently. One must particularly watch for the ability to laugh—nothing is more revealing than false attempts at laughter.

An additional maxim, then, as one ponders with whom one is going to identify politically: *Listen to their voices. Watch for the signals of compassion. Watch how they laugh.*

It is not all that difficult, in the end, to know with whom one belongs in the arena of political activity.

2. On Conservative Humanism

It is customary today to be asked, in a tone of truculent aggressiveness, "Whose side are you on?" The answer to this question, no matter who asks it, ought to be, *"Not yours, Mac!"* I shall return presently to what I consider to be a prime political imperative of our present situation —the refusal to identify with any horde. However, an individual may reasonably be asked to explain his overall presuppositions before one considers his specific views on the situation. In most cases, it may be assumed, there will be a connection between the two. For this reason I would like to state my general political position early in the game. This is a position of conservatism. More specifically, it is a position of conservative humanism.

I'm very much aware of the ambiguity of such political designations as "conservative," "liberal," or "radical," nor can I use this essay to attempt a systematic conceptual clarification. It remains true, though, that these broad designations refer to real differences in basic political outlook, even if they often fail to predict specific political opinions or stands. A preliminary and very simple definition of a conservative outlook, then, would be in terms of fundamental hesitation regarding social change. The prototypical conservative maxim can be put as follows: "Other things being equal, let society remain the way it is." Against this, both liberals and radicals share a propensity, a positive prejudice, toward change, the main difference between them being in the degree of change desired and in the amount of upheaval deemed acceptable in bringing change about. The prototypical maxim of the "left," be it liberal or radical in its particular coloration, can then be formulated: "Other things being equal, let society change." Now, it goes without saying that a lot will depend on just what things are considered to be equal or unequal. And it should also be stressed that there can be considerable agreement on this across the broad dividing lines, especially among individuals who share the motive of compassion (there are such individuals in almost all political camps). The dividing lines are still useful in giving a general idea where an individual stands on political matters.

Still speaking very broadly, there are two types of conservatives. The first are adversely disposed toward change because they consider the institutional arrangements of the *status quo* as being intrinsically good, natural, or even sacred. Any change in these arrangements, conversely, impresses them as evil, perverse, or even blasphemous. These are the conservatives by faith. Conservatives of the second type have a prejudice against change, *not* because they have profound convictions about the merits of the *status quo,* but because they have profound suspicions about the benefits of whatever is proposed as an alternative to the *status quo.* Pessimists and skeptics by inclination, these are the conservatives by lack of faith.

My own brand of conservatism puts me in this latter group. This is not unrelated to the fact that I'm a sociologist. There is a powerful debunking, disenchanting element about the perspective sociology. Consequently, as a sociologist, it is impossible for me to look at social institutions in the way that conservatives of the first group do. The same sociological perspective, however, induces skepticism about deliberate efforts to change society. Needless to say, such efforts must often be undertaken. But the sociologist will always be aware of what Max Weber called the unintended consequences of social action and others have called the irony of history. Social institutions are typically the result of accidents, not of deliberate design. Social institutions necessarily undergo change, but the direction of change is very hard to predict and even harder to control. If one wishes to change society, one ought to approach such a venture with the nervous care with which one would approach a particularly delicate and erratic piece of machinery. The enthusiast almost inevitably produces a mess of some sort. This is why the enthusiasm for change that characterizes both liberals and radicals, however admirable it may occasionally be in an individual personality, is a great danger in the realm of social institutions.

It should be emphasized that this brand of conservatism has very definite limits. It is a conservatism regarding political and institutional change. In other words, it does *not* derive from a philosophical or psychological commitment to immutability, but rather from empirical insight into the nature of socio-political reality. Thus this type of conservative outlook need not carry over at all into other areas of thought, into moral or aesthetic convictions, or into the manner in which an individual orders his private life. For example, an individual might well be a hard-shell conservative in politics, while at the same time his religious views are grossly heretical, his morals depraved and his views of art insane, in terms of the prevailing notions about these matters. In my own case, I carry no brief for conservatism in religion, in morality, or in aesthetics, and I see no contradiction whatever between my "radicalism" in some of these areas and my conservative predispositions in the socio-political sphere. There is, indeed, a connection between my religious and my political views, but it is indirect. I am a Christian and I am a conservative, but my conservatism does not derive from my Christianity, indeed would remain the same even if I were not a Christian (and *did* remain the same during a period of my life when I did not consider myself a Christian). Christianity, however, makes pessimism about human affairs easier to bear. This, incidentally, is an argument for *neither* Christianity *nor* conservatism, but it is a point that should at least be mentioned here.

What, then, are some basic orientations of this type of conservative?

A conservative accepts the messiness of history and is suspicious of the idea of progress. To accept the empirical reality of history as (most literally) a bloody mess is, of course, not to enjoy the spectacle. It is to learn how to live with it and how to reject the temptation to impose neat schemes on it. The idea of progress (in essence, the injection into history of a religious hope beyond history) is one of the neatest of these schemes. It is particularly dangerous because those who hold it usually think they, and only they, know exactly which way history is moving, and by virtue of this belief become inordinately arrogant and prone to sacrifice others on the altar of their alleged certainties. The conservative perspective on history, by contrast, lacks any such certainties, and especially the certainty that one is standing oneself in some particularly privileged position of access to the truth of history. The idea of progress typically invites this immodesty. To reject this idea does not, however, mean that history is a cycle of nights in which all cats are gray. There are, indeed, specific *progresses* in history, even if there is no one line of progress. Such *a* progress, for instance, has been the discovery of freedom in western history. Each such specific progress, however, may be lost again, destroyed, forgotten. A conservative perspective on history is, very deeply, a sense of its irony and its tragic content of human futilities.

A conservative is skeptical of innovation. He is doubly skeptical of violent innovation. To repeat, this skepticism is *not* based on a conviction that things are always best the way they are (obviously, this is rarely the case), but on empirical knowledge of what usually happens with the great innovations. At best, in most cases, the results turn out to be very different from those desired by the innovators. At worst, and this is often enough, people are worse off after the great innovation than they were before. This conservative skepticism applies particularly to the cataclysmic transformations of society commonly called revolutions. We shall return to this later.

A conservative accepts human beings as they are. As with the acceptance of the realities of history, this does not imply some wild enthusiasm about empirical man. Nor does it have to entail a theory about an allegedly immutable "human nature." It simply means a recognition of the limited capacity of man to transform himself radically. For this reason, a conservative will be moderate in what he expects of people. He will be deeply suspicious of all programs that presuppose or promise a "new man," especially as he is aware of the deplorable specimen that such programs have habitually come up with in the end. Conservatism is *humane* in the precise sense of the word, in that it predisposes one toward political courses of action that reckon with human beings as we know them, *not* with human beings projected by Utopian blueprints for the future. This humaneness in no way disparages the dignity and the courage of which men are capable. On the contrary, it respects these qualities as existing here and now, and *therefore* disdains the Utopian fantasies of those who cannot bear man as he is. Perhaps this has something to do with the ability to like people. If one really likes people (as against "loving mankind"), one will be much less disposed to talk of "radically transforming" them.

A conservative values order, continuity, and triviality in social life. Here particularly my perspective as a sociologist serves to undergird my political conservatism, but since this essay is not intended to be a sociological treatise I will resist the temptation to expound on these themes *qua* sociological theorist. Suffice it to say: Order is *the* fundamental social category. Any social relationship, and most emphatically any society that contains large numbers of people over time, is an imposition of order upon the spontaneous flux of individual activity. The most obvious, and also the most important, expression of this is the imposition of language upon experience. Without order there can be no shared meanings, no shared experiences, and ultimately no human life at all. Social institutions, in their essential character, are ordering structures and thus limits upon the spontaneity (if you will, the freedom) of the individual.

This does *not* mean that social order must be rigid or repressive—one look at language, the fundamental social institution, shows that this is not so. It does mean that societies can sustain only a certain measure of disorder before it becomes a direct threat to life itself—a threat against which societies will defend themselves instinctively (in the full sense of that word). It follows that any political ideology that elevates disorder to a moral principle is fundamentally anti-social—and anti-human.

Moreover, it is essential for human life that there be continuity in the social order. Only if there is continuity between past, present and future can the individual make sense of his own biography—and only society, through its institutions, can provide this continuity. This fundamental fact about social life, I would think, ought to be clear to anyone who has ever dealt seriously with children —and, by the way, it may not be an accident that those who make a cult of social discontinuity and disorder are rarely parents. It seems to me that no one who has ever been attentive to a child would take as ideal the murderous spontaneity of a world without social authority. Finally, it is essential for human life that a great part of social order be experienced as trivial—that is, as taken for granted with a minimum of reflection, as "uninteresting." Only against the background of triviality is there a possibility of individual ecstasy, drama, innovating thought or action. The attempt to imbue all social relations with profound "significance," and indeed to make all of life "interesting" is as destructive as it is doomed to fail. Social man requires triviality as urgently as biological man requires sleep. Contemporary radical thought that would do away with everything that is "dull" ("alienating," in current parlance) in society would, if successful, bring about a state of hell comparable to an unending night without sleep. Fortunately, such success is anthropologically impossible.

Now, these all too brief observations about order, continuity, and triviality could be developed theoretically at great length. Conservatives are rarely able to do this sort of theorizing, but they tend to have a healthy instinct about these things. This is why they respect what progressives of all stripes generally regard as "empty forms"— ceremony, ritual, manners, and all the "meaningless" traditions that give society a semblance of home.

A conservative is skeptical of grand intellectual designs for the improvement of society. This need not be "anti-intellectualism," in the sense of a disparagement of intellect and of men of ideas. Rather, it is doubt about the capacity of intellect to realize its projects in history and reluctance to let the men of ideas use history (that is, the lives of others) as an experimental laboratory. More deeply, this is related to what has just been said about triviality— namely, to the theory or the hunch, as the case may be, that too much consciousness is destructive of life. "Making conscious" (*Bewusstmachung* in German, *concientización* in Spanish) is today an important slogan of the New Left. Within certain limits, of course, this may refer to a worthwhile purpose—for example, making people conscious of the larger political or economic arrangements from which they suffer. If the slogan, however, is taken (as it often is) to denote a goal in which everyone, at all times, will consciously and deliberately "participate" in all the institutions of his society, then, once more, the vision evoked is one of hell. It would be the hell in which both sleep and dreaming have been murdered.

A conservative is skeptical of "movements." When masses of people are set in motion by a wave of political enthusiasm, the results are rarely what the movers had in mind and usually they are destructive. "Movements" are very able to tear down Bastilles, and once in a while this may be a good thing. "Movements" are hardly ever able to bring about lasting improvements in the quality of human life. It seems to me that nothing very decisive has been added to Gustave LeBon's insight that crowds act to destroy. It is all the more remarkable that intellectuals, whose education in the social sciences is formally impeccable, continue to be ready to fall into line with ever new mobilizations of crowds. Particularly ironic in this connection is that today many of those who enthusiastically surrender their will and reason to a new brand of horde mentality do so while mouthing Herbert Marcuse's slogan of "the great refusal." Marcuse, of course, had in mind refusing the conformism of "the system." Fine. Let me merely suggest that such refusal will gain credibility if it is coupled with a similar determination to refuse the conformism of whatever horde sets itself up as an anti-system. In other words, a conservative will be prepared, if necessary, to stand alone against what appears at any given moment as the "tide of history" or the "wave of the future." I hope that enough has been said before about compassion and about human solidarity to forestall the misunderstanding that what I have in mind here is a stance of self-satisfied isolation from the turmoil of the times.

A conservative is inclined to leave people alone. The type of conservatism that has been sketched here is marked by an awareness of historical relativity and, more deeply, by the ambiguities and the tragic dimensions of the human condition. It thus predisposes one toward modesty about the worth of one's style of life and one's own intellectual positions. The pragmatic corollary of such modesty is a tendency to let people live their own lives as they see fit, unless there are overwhelming reasons to override this tendency (reasons that, once more, must concern very concrete questions of human well-being). The liberal ideology of "development," which is causing so much havoc in the so-called Third World today, is a prime example of a contrary tendency. "Development" at first sounds like an unchallengeable boon. Upon closer examination one notices that the assumption is made that every society, from Papua to Paraguay, must go through certain pre-ordained steps to attain salvation—and, lo and behold, it usually turns out that these steps are those gone through by the "developed" society to which the particular theorist belongs.

Most radicals are just as bad. Again, there is piquant irony in the current slogan that "people have the right to control their own destiny"—a slogan habitually on the lips of individuals who are convinced that most of their contemporaries live lives of inauthenticity and worthlessness and that they, the sloganeers, have every right to interfere violently with this perfidious state of affairs. A conservative corrective to all this arrogance is a very simple translation to the political sphere of an old principle of good manners—to wit, that one not regale others with one's great wisdom unless one is asked. Incidentally, it was just this principle that made the much maligned British empire far superior morally (and, I suspect, polit-ically) to its American and Russian successors.

It goes without saying that what I have written here is not intended as an exhaustive exposition of a conserva-tive political philosophy. I hope that it has been sufficient to place within a broader perspective my opening ob-servations on political activity. Of necessity, this discus-sion has had to be fairly general, since the perspective applies to far more than the contemporary American situation, let alone the particular topic of contemporary American radicalism.

But what is the relevance of this perspective to the current situation?

The reader who has followed the preceding discussion with contemporary America at the back of his mind will already have made some pertinent applications. The rest of this essay will hopefully make a good many more. Another point that will already be evident is that the conservative humanism proposed here has little affinity with much that goes under the name of "conservatism" in America today. Much of this, when it is not a simple aversion to the upsetting of any social applecarts whatever, is a simplistic glorification of "Americanism" as a political creed. Upon closer inspection, the "Americanism" thus extolled is composed of an arrogant nationalism, a conviction of the ultimate rectitude of republican institutions, and a blind faith in the superiority of capitalism. Far from being in the conservative tradition of, say, Edmund Burke or Alexis de Tocqueville (both of whom, in addition to Max Weber, I would count among the intellectual mentors of my type of conservatism), this ideology is actually a fixation on certain socio-political innovations of the nineteenth century—in this, incidentally, it is not too different from the Marxist ideology that plays the role of devil in its world. I find myself much closer in my thinking to, for instance, Metternich, who understood (quite correctly, I believe) that nationalism and mass democracy were the twin fruits of the modern revolutionary impetus—and that both were very dubious innovations indeed. It is possible to love one's country and to adhere to its basic political institutions without idolizing either. As to capitalism, I regard it as demonstrably superior in economic efficacy to any of its currently available alternatives, at any rate in the developed countries, but this does not prevent me from seeing its social inequities or from questioning some of the values it has engendered. In brief, the very last thing I have in mind is to present the reader with an ideology that would glorify America or to invite him into a "conservative movement."

"Whose side are you on?" "Not yours, Mac—*and not that of any other horde, either.*"

"Great refusal?" Yes. Of "the system"—whenever it tramples upon human beings. Of any horde, whether it calls itself "left," "right," or upside-down—whenever *it* falls prey to the language and the gestures of inhumanity.

Very simple political maxims: Learn how to refuse the existing orthodoxies. Learn also how to refuse the would-be orthodoxies of tomorrow. Participate in the lives of others, but think your own thoughts. Accept "alienation"—it is the price of freedom. *Learn how to stand apart.*

I know full well that this is not a message with which one is likely to gain popularity. Especially not among young people, who need warmth—be it the warmth provided by "the establishment" or the warmth of the rebel band. I'm under no illusion, therefore, that the kind of perspective I have proposed here could be the foundation of a political "movement" of any kind—nor, obviously, would I welcome this.

This essay, then, does not propose a political program. Any such program must strive to inspire large masses of people. What I have to say, alas, is not terribly inspiring. I can address myself only to individuals. I don't know how many individuals there are to whose concerns it is capable of speaking. I do know that there are some, including some who have been among my students. These are the individuals who, moved to political activity by the outrages of our time, are yet determined not to be seduced by the clamor of ideologies. Nor, to be sure, do I want to seduce them . . .

But no. That last sentence was less than honest. I visualize the individuals I have in mind and I must confess that, yes, I do want to seduce them. If, that is, it is possible to seduce by compassion and by reason.

3. On "The Movement"

It is evident that people speaking about "The Movement" in America today have different things in mind. "The Movement" means opposition to the war in Vietnam and to the arms race, a concern for human rights abroad and at home, and a particular identification with the aspirations of American Negroes. In other words, "The Movement" seems to be about specific social and political issues of the time. But "The Movement" also seems to be about sexual emancipation, about the "generation gap," about a new style of life which, ranging from its religious interests to its taste in music, stands in self-conscious tension with prevailing middle-class culture. In other words, "The Movement" appears to have some relationship to bohemian nonconformity. This is all more than a little confusing—even to individuals who regard themselves as being within "The Movement." After all, it is not immediately clear how the demand "Stop the War in Vietnam!" relates to such other demands as "Legalize Pot!" or "Student Power!" I think, therefore, that it is necessary to gain greater clarity about just what "The Movement" is before one can make any kind of intelligent political judgment about it. For me, at any rate, such clarification means to place the phenomenon within a sociological perspective.

The crucial clue to the nature of "The Movement" is the fact that its adherents are mainly young. More specifically, "The Movement" has an important relation to what is now commonly called the youth culture. To be sure, the two phenomena are by no means coextensive. There are older and emphatically "square" people associated with the political causes espoused by "The Movement." And there are broad segments of the youth culture in which there is only minimal interest in these or any other political issues. All the same, there is a continuity of reactive patterns, of mood and of life styles between these two phenomena. I don't think that this is accidental or superficial.

I believe that one ought to distinguish between three related but distinct entities—*youth culture, youth movements,* and *radical movements.* If one is addicted to graphic representation, one may picture these as three overlapping circles, with only a relatively small area being part of all of them.

The first entity, youth culture, is the broadest of these phenomena. It is to be found today in all advanced industrial societies, and it has, in my opinion, deep roots in the fundamental structures of these societies. I'm convinced that youth culture will continue to be an important and durable feature in these societies.

The second entity, that of youth movements, represents an *ad hoc* activation of the youth culture around some issues about which its members are concerned. It is very important to see that these issues do not necessarily have to be political in character. Youth movements of some sort are likely to appear from time to time, at least until the youth culture has attained firm institutional forms that will "freeze" or at least channel its more spontaneous expressions.

The third entity, that of radical movements, is at the moment in a state of tenuous symbiosis with the much broader youth context. There is the attempt (very conscious and deliberate in the case of the radical groups on university campuses) to activate segments of the youth culture for the purpose of revolutionarily transforming the larger society. At least as far as America is concerned, I don't expect this attempt to be successful and I would not predict a very bright future for the movements in question.

What are some of the important sociological features of the youth culture?

The structural trends of advanced industrial societies that underlie the phenomenon are fairly clear by now. In the main, youth culture has been produced, or at least made possible, by the combination of two trends—a shift in the demographic constitution of modern societies and a shift in the demands of the labor market. Largely as a result of modern medical technology, the proportion of young people in the population has been growing. And, as a result of the technological character of modern economies, the bulk of these young people are kept out of the productive process for ever longer periods of time —partly because there is no need for all this manpower, partly because what manpower is needed is deemed to require increasingly long periods of educational preparation. What has come about, in consequence, is a lengthening period of "youth," understood by the society as a biographical stage between "childhood" and "maturity" (I put these terms in quotation marks because there is nothing sociologically or biologically necessary about them). But the society has as yet only very unclear notions about the proper purposes, the rights and obligations, and even the institutional forms of this stage in life. The contemporary "youth crisis" is a simple function of this unclearness. In other words, there now exists a gap between the structural facts and the cultural definition of "youth." Contemporary youth culture is an initially spontaneous creation of those having to live in this gap, an attempt to provide the cultural definitions that the larger society has failed to come up with. The contemporary youth crisis is essentially a "bargaining process" between the youth culture and the larger society—one in which, I think, the youth culture is progressively successful in getting general acceptance for its self-definitions.

These features of the youth culture have often been

remarked upon, and there is a wide consensus that something like the process just described is taking place. However, there is another dimension to the phenomenon that,
to my knowledge, has not been noticed. The youth culture
is not only between childhood and maturity in the chrono-
logical sense. It is also between the values and the forms
of consciousness that dominate these two biographical
stages in modern societies. More specifically, youth culture
is located at the point of conflict between the ethos of
modern childhood and the ethos of modern bureaucracy.
I believe that a better understanding of this conflict, and
of its profound roots in modern society, is very important
if greater clarity is to be gained on what goes on in the
world today. I must be very brief about this here, but I
would like at least to point to this dimension, germane as
it is to the subject of this essay.

A plausible argument can be made that one of the pro-
foundest transformations of the modern world has been
the transformation of childhood. The demographic features of this transformation are the abrupt decline in
child mortality and the shrinkage in family size. The most
important structural feature is the separation (physical
and in terms of values) of the family, and thus of childhood, from the productive process. Concomitant with
these features there has developed a new cultural conception of childhood, arising first in the bourgeoisie and then
spreading out until today it embraces most of the society.
This new conception has given an importance to childhood
that, at least in western cultures, it has never had before. Very probably all this has meant that childhood
today is more protected and just plain happier than it
has ever been before. Previously, most children died within
the first few years of their lives. Today, most children
grow to maturity. One has to grasp the emotional consequences that this transformation has had *for parents*
if one is to understand its staggering significance. Probably for the first time in human history, when a child is
born today, the parents can bestow love on this child

without having to reckon with the probability that, in the very near future, their grief will be all the more bitter for it. There is a new emotional calculus along with the new demographic one—and it is important to recall that all of this is very recent indeed.

Of equal importance are the somewhat older features of family size and of the separation of childhood from the "serious" world of work. The former has meant that each child can make claims upon the attention of his elders that were physically impossible in the large family. The latter has located childhood in a social sphere that is very much protected from the uglier and more violent conflicts of social life. In this connection it should also be mentioned that modern childhood is largely protected from the experiences of painful illness and of death. Within this physical and social setting the modern child, not surprisingly, comes to feel very early that he is a person of considerable importance. He learns that he has a dignity and rights that belong to him as a unique individual. He also learns that society (that is, the elders who serve as "administrators" of the world of childhood) is pliant and responsive to all his needs. Typically, he acquires a low frustration threshold.

One way of putting this would be to say that modern childhood produces "soft" individuals. But the word "soft" has an overly negative connotation in our language —no doubt a linguistic carry-over from a time when childhood and its educational ideals were much harsher than they are today. I prefer speaking of all this by using the more positive term of humaneness. Childhood today is vastly more humane than it was before, and it brings forth more humane individuals. If they are "softer" in having less tolerance for frustration, they are also "softer" in being less tolerant of callousness and cruelty in human relations. I'm willing to take the "softness" as a fair price for the latter. I would like to emphasize, then, that I see the consequences of modern childhood as very largely positive. Quite apart from its consequences, I see the discovery of childhood by modern society as one of its most significant human achievements. Thus I'm reassured by the sociological insight that this achievement is rooted in some of the basic structures of modern society—and is thus unlikely to be lost again in the foreseeable future.

It is all the more important to see the conflict with another deeply rooted fact of modern society, one equally unlikely to pass away—that of modern bureaucracy. Again, this is not the place to expound what sociologists have found out about bureaucracy. Suffice it to say that, like it or not, bureaucratic forms of administration are inevitable in a modern society, both because of its mass population and because of its complex technology. If bureaucracy vanished from America tomorrow, not only would our lives be thrown into immeasurable chaos, but most of us would literally die. The critics of bureaucracy generally think about the Pentagon or, at best, the Registrar's Office. They habitually overlook the fact that food supply, garbage collection, and basic utilities also require bureaucratic administrations, which actually are not all that different in appearance from those of the military or the educational establishment. Bureaucracy, however, is more than a form of administration. It also has an ethos—and, very probably, that ethos is endemic to it. The ethos has various features—such as orderliness, punctuality, concern for detail, and the like. Its most important feature in terms of human relations, however, is impersonality. Of necessity, bureaucratic administration fosters impersonality. Indeed, it fosters impersonality as a value. It administers its jurisdiction, whatever that may be, "without regard to persons." "Personal influence" or "personal attachments" are vices, *not* virtues, in the bureaucratic universe. Since modern bureaucracies administer people as well as things, and vast numbers of people at that, it is quite inevitable that the individual will be "treated as a number." Adjustment to a bureaucratically run society involves the capacity to treat others, and toleration of being treated oneself, in an impersonal way.

These are the outlines of the conflict. Modern childhood is marked by values and by a consciousness that are emphatically personalistic. Modern bureaucracy, by contrast, has an ethos of emphatic impersonality. Put simply, an individual shaped by modern childhood is most likely to feel oppressed by modern bureaucracy. Indeed, he is likely to have a very low "oppression threshold" when it comes to the impersonal procedures of bureaucracy. Thus people today feel oppressed, "alienated" or even "exploited" simply by being subjected to bureaucratic processes (say, by a university administration) that a generation ago would simply have been accepted as pragmatic necessities. Any process in which the individual is "treated as a number," even if the process is set in motion for indisputably benign purposes, is experienced as an offense to human dignity. Not surprisingly, the bureaucracy of the educational establishment bears the brunt of this outrage today, since it is, for obvious reasons, the *first* bureaucracy that most individuals come across in their lives.

On one level, of course, this outrage is absurd. There is nothing intrinsically evil about the bureaucratic ethos, not even about individuals being "treated as numbers" for specific, limited and morally unobjectionable purposes. On this level, then, one might say that the conflict between the values of the modern nursery and the values of the Bell Telephone System will have to be resolved by people "growing up" and accepting their area codes as a fact of life. But things are not all that simple. In addition to the absurdity there is also a very healthy moral instinct in the anti-bureaucratic animus. There is, after all, the knowledge that people can be numbered for killing and for being killed by bureaucracies as efficient and as streamlined as those of an American public utility. There is, after all, the bureaucracy of the Selective Service System as well as that of Bell Telephone. There are area codes of death, bureaucratically administered—just think of a map of Vietnam laid out on a Pentagon planning desk. There is, therefore, another level of this conflict that I suggest

we take with great moral seriousness—namely, the protest against bureaucratized inhumanity—and positively, by
demanding that all bureaucracies be in the service of
man and not of his destruction.

It seems to me that the phenomenon of contemporary
youth culture can be understood much more clearly against
this background, which, I think, sharply illuminates some
of its most conspicuous themes. The youth culture is
strongly communalistic, always in quest of what sociologists call *Gemeinschaft.* At the same time, it extols the
individual, his right to live as he chooses, to "do his thing."
The communalism and the individualism are in a certain
tension with each other, and in fact the youth culture has
tended to produce tribalistic congregations in which individual nonconformity is minimized or, more precisely, in-
verted in false consciousness into a collective ritual. Yet
there is an underlying logic in the combination. Both the
communalism and the individualism imply a peculiarly
modern notion of identity—to wit, the notion of identity
not as given but as progressively acquired by the individual, with various communities (mostly, of course, communities of peers) functioning as enabling contexts for the
acquisition of identity.

Put differently, the communities of the young provide
"identity workshops" for individuals in search of themselves, and the youth culture as a whole represents a
permanent institutionalization of "identity crisis." It is important to understand that it can fulfill this function (probably one of great importance in our fragmented society)
despite the faddish and transitory quality of many of its
specific contents—different identities appear on the "market," sometimes following rapid changes in supply and demand, but the social mechanisms by which these identities
are distributed and "consumed" remain quite constant.
Thus the youth culture can have a rapid turnover of specific aesthetic, ideological or political "materials," while
continuing to function as the social context within which
individuals "find themselves."

Personalistic values are given top place in the moral hierarchy of the youth culture. Such values are "sincerity," "sensitivity," "responsiveness," and general openness to others and to new experiences. Related to this is the sensualism of the youth culture, expressed most forcefully in its ecumenical tolerance for sexual options of every conceivable sort, expressed more marginally (and possibly less lastingly) in its interest in psychedelic drugs and religious mysticism. Running strongly through all this are as yet rather diffuse themes that can, however, be called the incipient elements of a new humanism. This is expressed negatively in youth's opposition to all social structures that are conceived as inhuman, "repressive," "life-denying," and positively in a radical egalitarianism (between the sexes *and* the different modes of sexual expression, between races and nationalities), an openness toward political movements of "liberation" of all kinds (imagined as well as real), and in the most general theme of "solidarity," as a universal empathy with all sorts and conditions of men.

The youth culture is only now in process of formation. Some of its characteristics have not yet settled down into durable cultural forms. Some of its institutions are just beginning to emerge. Nor is it clear at this moment just how the eventual result of the "bargaining process" between youth culture and larger society will look, though some features of the accommodation are beginning to be visible (for example in the university, which, above all, is likely to emerge as *the* institutional locus of the youth culture—much to my regret, incidentally). All the same, I would reiterate my conviction that the youth culture is the matrix and the broadest social base for a number of humanization impulses in modern society—and is thus, whatever reservations one may have about some of its features, one of the more hopeful phenomena of our time. "The Movement" may then, at least in part, be understood in terms of these impulses toward humanization, as a movement partly *of* the youth culture and partly (what-

ever its other origins) using it as its most promising constituency. Related as it is to the aforementioned global
trends, "The Movement" in this sense is likely to be a
continuing or recurring phenomenon in American society
and on the American political scene. To the extent that
at least one of the motives strongly present in it is the
motive of compassion with others, the prognosis is com-
forting.

"The Movement," however, is today also associated with
political radicalism, especially with the New Left, in the
minds of both many of its adherents and many of its
enemies. I believe that this association will turn out to
be transitory, largely because I don't expect the New Left
to continue as an important phenomenon in America. But
since the association is of some importance at this moment, especially in the context of radical movements among
students, it has to be taken into account.

Student radicalism, and the New Left in general, are
also, of course, movements of considerable heterogeneity
—in ideology, in tactics and in life styles. Among "student
radicals" we find doctrinaire Marxists and those contemptuous of any ideological formulation, pacifists and do-it-
yourself producers of Molotov cocktails, denizens of sex
communes and would-be ascetics. I believe that it is quite
futile to attempt a coherent typology of this confused
scenery. Rather, the phenomenon of student radicalism
becomes understandable if one sees it, primarily, as an
invasion of the university by the youth culture—or, put
differently, a movement of the youth culture designed to
transform the university into its own institutional mold.
Seen in this fashion, the political characteristics of most
of this movement are haphazard and ephemeral. They
are "left" today, but could just as easily be "right" tomorrow—or, more plausibly, any political coloration may
fade away completely.

As a movement arising out of the youth culture, student
radicalism shares many of its broad characteristics—the
communalistic nostalgia, the aversion to discipline and bu-

reaucratic structures, and certainly the deeply running humanistic impulse. All the same, within this movement there is also something else—a core of ideologically set political radicals, also split within themselves into competing sects (some explicitly Marxist, preponderantly of Maoist or Castrist persuasion, others standing more or less clearly in an anarchist-syndicalist tradition), but all united in the conviction that they are the vanguard of a coming American revolution. It is this radical core, of course, that successfully draws mass-media attention to itself in any local campus crisis, and that has been able to *épater les bourgeois* to such an extent (a somewhat ironic term, come to think of it, since this is a radical movement whose leadership and constituency are monolithically bourgeois themselves).

This radical movement, then, has a complex relationship to the youth culture. It is a relationship with elements of symbiosis and alliance, but also of conflict. There is a symbiotic merging of Utopian urges and communal experiences of solidarity (typically, solidarity *against* representatives of adult bureaucracy and "repression"). There are efforts of deliberate alliance, with the political radicals (often tongue-in-cheek) trying to capitalize on "issues" generated by the youth culture, such as demands for a relaxation of university rules on private behavior. But there is also real conflict. The sensualism, the cult of experience and the easygoing tolerance of the youth culture impinge negatively on the radicals' need for ideological definitions. Anti-authoritarianism and aversion to discipline are fine if directed against the enemy, as ideologically defined, but can be a big nuisance within the radical movement itself. Most importantly, the humanistic impulses of the youth culture can be mobilized for radical purposes, dramatically so in the opposition to the war, but the same impulses become a danger when the radicals themselves start to advocate or even practice violence of dubious humanitarian sensitivity. Put simply, "soft" people are easy marks for

revolutionary rhetoric, but very poor material for the formation of revolutionary cadres.

While I'm quite confident about the social causes and
dynamics of the youth culture, I'm not so sure why the
New Left, especially in its student movement, has exploded
so powerfully on the American scene in recent years. The
"obvious" explanation, that the cause lies in the deplorable
performance of America in Vietnam and elsewhere, loses
plausibility as soon as one reflects that student radicalism,
like the youth culture, is an international phenomenon.
One can understand why students at Berkeley are "radicalized" because of Vietnam and because of Watts. But why
in Amsterdam and in Frankfurt? I'm quite sure that any
specific national "issue" raised by the radicals at a given
moment is fortuitous, if it is not deliberately selected as
a strategy. None of these "issues" explain the motives of
the would-be revolutionaries and often not even of those
they succeed in mobilizing. It follows, by the way, that
the liberal belief that radicals can be assuaged by meeting
their demands on this or that "issue" is an illusion. I
strongly suspect that, as very often in history, there is an
element of sheer accident in the "leftward" turn of the
effervescence present among students in America (and, for
that matter, in western Europe). If there is any rational
cause, it probably has something to do with America, but
I doubt if it is as simple as moral outrage against American actions in Vietnam or in the racial situation. More
likely, it is the sheer presence of the American empire,
serving as an irresistible focus for anti-authoritarian and
anti-*status-quo* hostilities of every kind. In other words, I
suspect that it is American power much more than American immoralities that has given the political coloration of
"left" to rebellious students. This still, however, leaves
open the possibility that the massive collapse in the plausibility of American political ideals as a result of Vietnam
may have served as an important contributing factor.

Whatever the causes, the political radicalism has become
a factor in the "bargaining process" between the youth

culture and the larger society. It is important to see it for what it is and to decide how to respond to it. I must confess that it took me some time to understand this myself. While I have never had any sympathies for "left" ideologies, I found myself agreeing with student radicals about a number of "issues," notably on the war and on black emancipation, and I was prepared to dismiss their ideological rhetoric as being of minor importance. I still feel that it *is* of minor importance for most participants in "The Movement," who are basically moved by humane impulses and who are caught (if at all) in the radical rhetoric largely because no one has presented them with more challenging ideas. But, I have had to conclude that the ideology is indeed important for the core of politically committed radicals, the sort of individuals who provide the leadership of Students for a Democratic Society and similar groups. And I have had to conclude further that the designation "left" is generally misleading in this context and that the ideology in fact bears a striking resemblance to that of early fascism, in both its Italian and German varieties.

It might be worthwhile to mention the experiences that led me to this conclusion. It was not, at first, a matter of intellectually analyzing the ideological contents. What happened first was that, in conversations about the war, I realized that my opposition had really nothing to do with the radicals. *My* opposition was based on such simple (to them, of course, simplistic) convictions as that it is wrong to drop napalm on villages inhabited by children. *Their* opposition was not to napalm-dropping at all—it was to "American imperialism." Indeed, they had no objection at all to acts of violence that killed children, even with deliberation—as long as it was the "right people," from their viewpoint, that did the killing. I still recall vividly a conversation wth a radical type of some philosophical ability, in which he explained to me very patiently (after all, I was politically naïve) that the act of torturing a prisoner to death by an insurgent was a totally (he said, an "anthropologically") different thing from the same act performed by a member of counterinsurgency forces. I began to take a sharper look at this radical ideology once I grasped the principle of selectivity in its humanistic rhetoric. Another kind of experience was more closely linked to my own biography. As I was observing the radicals in action, their language and their gestures, I was repeatedly reminded of the stormtroopers that marched through my childhood in Europe. I first dismissed this association as subjective, perhaps even neurotic. Perhaps, I thought, all intense political activism has these traits. But when, for example, I thought of Communist (*Old* Left) activists I have had occasion to observe, I realized that, although I had no affection for them either, they did *not* arouse these particular associations. It was at this point that I turned to systematic reflection about the new radical ideology, which led me to the conclusion that the ideology was much less new than it first seemed and that the resemblance to some vivid memories of my childhood was not all that subjective after all.

What is specifically fascist about this ideology?

A movement characterized by its negations rather than by a positive vision of the future: The new radicals take it as *ipso-facto* evidence of counterrevolutionary intellectualism if one asks specific questions about their design for the future. The old radicals (and this, let there be no mistake about it, is how the early fascists conceived of themselves) had an identical contempt for "empty intellectual criticisms." In this connection it is highly instructive that the attack by contemporary American radicals on value-free sociology follows step by step the earlier attack of Nazi ideologists on the same conception of the discipline —both, interestingly, using the designation "positivistic" for any social scientist not committed in his work to their respective political visions.

The specific combination of negations—anti-stability, anti-liberal, anti-capitalist, and anti-intellectual: Stability, especially the stability of the bureaucratic state and of bourgeois society, is an evil in itself. The basic counter-position is between "the movement" (*die Bewegung,* as the Nazis called themselves) and "the system" (*das System,* as they called the Weimar Republic and its society)—the one absolutely noble and embodying the wave of the future, the other absolutely corrupt and representing nothing but decaying stasis. The radical is the anti-type of the bourgeois (the "square" today, *der Spiesser* yesterday). Liberal democracy is a sham and, indeed, is the principal enemy. Capitalism is intrinsically wicked and must be replaced by a form of economy in which collective solidarity takes precedence over predatory individualism. Rationality is nothing but manipulation on behalf of "the system." Furthermore, the emotional context within which these negations are proclaimed is one of hatred and rage.

The cult of action for its own sake and the faith in the therapeutic value of violence: Today these themes are legitimated by a murky mixture of existentialism (Sartre filtered through Fanon) and Third World revolutionary romanticism. Yesterday the same themes found ideological justification in the poetic *dinamismo* of d'Annunzio and the romantic glorification of war as the "bath of steel" that purifies men. The clearest symptom of the continuity of these themes is the mystique of the street. I recall a recent scene I watched on television, a group of students chanting rhythmically, "The streets belong to the people"— and the almost physical shock as I remembered, at this moment, the opening lines of the second verse of the "Horst Wessel Lied," the anthem of the Nazi movement— *"Die Strasse frei den braunen Bataillonen . . ."*—"Clear the streets for the brown battalions . . ."

The political cult of youth: How, in the midst of all the glorification of youth that surrounds us today, could one forget that the anthem of Mussolini's Italy began with the invocation *"Giovinezza, giovinezza, primavera di bellezza . . ."*—"Youth, youth, springtime of beauty . . ."? Indeed, youth always and plausibly represents

energy, vigor, and vistas of the future. But its political
idolization need not necessarily bring about a "springtime
of beauty."

The totalization of friend and foe, and the concomitant
dehumanization of the latter: Again, linguistic usage is
highly instructive here. Anyone who remembers the Nazi
usage of *Saujuden* should stop to reflect about the human
implications of the current usage of the term "pigs." But
even those with shorter memories should be aware of the
fact that, by definition, pigs are designated for slaughter.

Finally, the assurance of the radicals that they represent
a mystical "general will," even though it is undiscoverable
by empirical means: In other words, there is a mystical
elitism that links the older and the new radicalism. This
elitism is particularly repulsive in view of the democratic
rhetoric of the latter. In fact, the new radicals are not
only contemptuous of the mechanisms of liberal parlia-
mentary democracy; they are fundamentally contemptuous
of *any* procedures designed to find out what people want
for themselves. The radicals don't have to find out what
I want—they already know what is good for me. What
this elitism means in practice can be readily grasped by
watching the manipulations of any SDS group on an
American campus.

If one adds up these themes, one is confronted by an
ideological constellation that strikingly resembles the common core of Italian and German fascism. Indeed, one
is drawn to the conclusion that the concepts and interpretations drawn by many contemporary radicals from Marxism are grafted upon a body of motives and perspectives
on the world that have nothing to do with Marxism. The
same conclusion, incidentally, has been arrived at by some
Marxists. But what is missing in the parallelism between
these two radicalisms?

Two themes are missing today—nationalism and the
authoritarian "leadership principle" (*Fuehrerprinzip*). I
would not want to dismiss this too lightly. For one thing,

the anti-nationalism and the anti-authoritarianism of the new radicalism still permit its adherents some degree of openness to the humanistic impulses emanating from the youth culture (a *mutual* openness, to boot). But I would also point out that the new radicals have shown a considerable capacity for what could be called vicarious nationalism. In America this has primarily taken the form of uncritical identification with black nationalism, an identification that (significantly) has not shrunk even from its anti-Semitic undertones. In America and elsewhere there has also been a vicarious solidarity with the virulent nationalisms of the Third World. Thus, there have been certain substitutes for the fascist *Volk* mystique. As to the anti-authoritarianism of the new radicals, I don't have too much confidence in its durability. I'm inclined to think that a charismatic leader with some organizational ability and a cynical attitude toward the democratic rhetoric of the radicals would have little difficulty overcoming their aversion to "authority figures."

What, of course, is also different between the older and the new radicalism is the general political context, and therefore the chances of political success. Fascism in Italy and in Germany had a ready social base in the seething caldron of an impoverished and resentful lower middle class. It was on the tide of *petit-bourgeois* hatred and ambition that the fascist movement rode into power (although once in power, of course, it did little enough in the interest of its original clientele). This social base not only does not exist for the new radicalism, but is already being effectively mobilized against it. The new radicalism, in both its constituency and its outlook, is emphatically *upper*-middle-class, and it is emphatically resented as such by the masses of the *petite bourgeoisie* and working class both. Its efforts to attract sympathy in these classes have been pathetically unsuccessful. This is as true in western Europe as in America. There have, indeed, been some alliances in America between the radicals and black militants, but I strongly suspect that these will turn out to be very transitory. Black militancy, despite the rhetorical fantasies engaged in by some of its intellectuals, is essentially a realistic bid for power and privilege *within* the context of the American social order. It is too realistic to associate itself durably with the aspirations of those who, with so little power at their disposal, would like to overthrow that social order. Thus the attempts to enlist working-class sympathies and to "unleash" the black masses are both rooted, I believe, in illusion. The only masses that the new radicals have the remotest chance of "unleashing" are college students and perhaps some other sectors of the youth culture (notably high school students). This potential social base, however, is also likely to shrink as the youth culture as a whole is increasingly victorious in its "bargaining process" with the larger society. Put differently, an educational establishment already "taken over" by the youth culture is going to be an increasingly unlikely candidate to be "taken over" by radical movements.

The political significance of the new radicalism, therefore, is in terms not so much of its intrinsic dangerousness as of its capacity to mobilize a political reaction against it. I don't share the apocalyptic visions of a coming American totalitarianism of the "right" that some liberals conjure up in this context. Barring presently unforeseen disasters on the international scene or within the American economy, I don't see very much likelihood of such totalitarian developments. But what I do see is that the highly conspicuous turmoil produced by the radicals will bring in an era of "law and order" politics of the kind we are already experiencing. What is bad about this politics is not its emphasis on lawful and orderly social processes, but its negative response to social change of any kind. "Law and order," with much waving of flags, can then become a simple smokescreen for "business as usual." In the present American situation, however, such politics is a recipe for disaster. We very badly need some far-reaching changes in both our foreign and domestic policies. The radicals are a danger principally because they can give the society a plausible alibi for leaving things just as they are. It seems to me that conservatives, above all, should be wary of falling into this trap of political psychology. There are very good political reasons, therefore, for having no truck with the extreme radicals. But I hope that I have said enough to indicate that I have better and more personal reasons. I don't want to have any truck with them because what they have to offer offends both reason and compassion.

What, then, of "The Movement"?

It is not unique in history in being a mixture of the admirable and the repulsive. Within it, *even within the ambience of the new radicalism,* there are authentic humanistic impulses that offer great hope. I think that one ought to welcome these impulses and to associate oneself with the specific political causes in which they find expression. Within it, too, however, there is a good deal of foolishness and some penetrating ugliness, and not only among the radicals. I see no reason for closing one's eyes to these aspects. Most importantly, anyone who identifies himself as a humanist (be it "conservative," "liberal," or "radical") ought to be at all times vigilant against the "selective humanism" that condemns the atrocities of one side while ignoring or even extolling those of the other side. Indeed, "selective humanism" in this sense is one of the best negative tests I know for making moral judgments in the political sphere. I hope that it will increasingly be applied by a generation that is as determinedly moralistic as this one —even if the price is having to fight on more than one front at a time.

4. On Revolution—
Rhetorical and Real

Revolution talk is in fashion today, especially among the young and among intellectuals. Che Guevara rivals the latest rock stars in producing hysteria among teen-agers. College rebels perceive administration buildings as the foot-hills of the Sierra Maestra. And middle-aged readers of *The New York Review* get a brief lease on spiritual potency by empathizing with the Vietcong. We even have professors now who want to liberate sociology and bishops who have discovered Jesus as a premature Black Panther.

Most of this is quite harmless. Children don't become terrorists by having posters of revolutionaries, just as they don't become militarists by playing with toy soldiers. Anyone who sees the capture of a dean as equivalent to the fall of Havana is probably badly in need in some sort of reassurance, and in most cases one might not want to begrudge him the pleasure. As to middle-aged intellectuals, one is inclined to let them find their orgasms where they can. All of this is in the sphere of games and of psychotherapy. It becomes relevant in the political sphere when significant numbers of people begin to take it seriously. At least among students this is the case today. It is therefore necessary to speak to the topic politically.

First of all, I would suggest a clarification of usage. Obviously the term "revolution" can be used with different meanings. We speak of the French Revolution and of the Industrial Revolution. We speak of the revolution in sales techniques in a certain firm or of a particular novel as producing a literary revolution. Even in the context of politics we use the term "revolutionary" to apply, say, to the civil rights movement or the "new politics" within the Democratic Party, while at the same time applying it to guerrilla movements in the Third World. There is nothing intrinsically bad about such broad usage; everyday language would be awful if it followed the precise distinctions of the logician. Thus I have no interest in polemicizing against a usage that applies the term "revolution" to any phenomenon of rapid or far-reaching change. But if one tries to think about politics with some intellectual rigor—and I think that this is urgently necessary today— then one ought to watch one's language with some care. I suggest that the term "revolution" be limited to those situations in which the attempt is made to effect fundamental social or political change by means of armed force. This limitation will allow us to know exactly what we are speaking about, without in any way excluding or prejudging other situations to which the term is loosely applied.

Revolution, in this sense, is a desperately serious business wherever it is a present or imminent reality. It is desperately serious because, like war, it involves questions of life and death, of killing and of being killed. The revolutionary romanticism that is currently in fashion is unserious precisely because it obfuscates the brutal reality of revolution and thus evades the moral questions that revolution raises. The reality of revolution, as against the romantic fantasies about it, is as ugly as the reality of war, and in some instances it is uglier. Like other kinds of war, revolution means the mutilation and death of human beings, combatants and noncombatants alike. It means shattered lives, devastated homes, grief and despair. But there is also a peculiar ugliness to revolutionary warfare, an ugliness in which, in most cases, both the revolutionaries and those arrayed against them fully participate. Revolution means bombs thrown into crowded cafes, throats slit in the dark of night, men and women lined up for

execution before roadside ditches. Revolution means the
indiscriminate bombing of villages, the taking of hostages,
the torture of prisoners. To be sure, there have been revolutionaries (Guevara was one of them) who sought to miti-
gate the inhumanity—just as there have been experts in
counterinsurgency warfare who have tried the same thing.
The record, however, hardly bears them out. On the contrary, it suggests that terror and counterterror are well-
nigh inevitable in this sort of warfare, and that those who
would like to see it otherwise (regardless of whether this
is because they have human scruples or because they regard brutality as "counterproductive") usually end up by
bowing to the grim realism of the situation.

The revolutionary romanticism of today is severely
guilty of selective humanism in its approach to these matters. The perceptions of Cuba and of Vietnam by our
radicals are the most relevant case in point. As modern
revolutions go, the Cuban one was relatively humane. Yet,
according to its own figures, the revolutionary regime executed well over a thousand individuals after it came to
power—most of them amid mob scenes of hysterical bes-
tiality, the same scenes in which the shout "Up against
the wall!" still fashionable among our radicals, hounded
human beings to their death. The judgment of relative
humaneness hardly fits the Vietnamese revolution. By
reliable estimates, about one hundred thousand people
were massacred after Ho Chi Minh came to power in the
north. As to the revolutionaries in the south, their standard
operating procedures not only include the public torture
and execution of individuals they suspect of being opposed
to them, but also the killing and sometimes the mutilation
of members of these individuals' families. This roll of horror also runs in the tens of thousands.

I want there to be no ambiguity whatever about the
reason I cite these facts. It is *not* to deny, in the Cuban
case, that the Batista regime was corrupt and itself guilty
of vile atrocities. It is certainly *not* to assert, in the case
of Vietnam, that the crimes perpetrated by the other side

are in any way a justification for those perpetrated by ourselves and by the regime we have kept in power. Indeed, in the case of Vietnam, there is good moral reason for being concerned, first and foremost, with the inhumanity for which we, as a nation, are responsible. But this is no reason for ignoring or justifying the inhumanity of the others. Only those who have learned to look steadily at *all* the human suffering brought about by revolution have any chance of making moral judgments on the subject that are something else than rationalizations of horror.

Nevertheless, despite all this, it is necessary to reaffirm that there is a right to revolution. This right is present in situations where human suffering from the *status quo* is so great that it appears just to accept the price in suffering that will have to be paid in overthrowing the *status quo*. Even then, however, this right is not to be exercised lightly. It ought to be very clear that there is, indeed, a reasonable chance that the suffering of the present will be mitigated in the post-revolutionary situation—in other words, it ought to be clear not only that the revolution has a chance to succeed, but that it has a chance to accomplish its goals in the wake of its victory. It ought also to be very clear that the recourse to revolutionary violence is the very last resort that is reasonably available. And even then there is never the implication that, because the revolution is right, it is also right to use all and any means to accomplish it. Just as the only possible justification for revolution is compassion, so the only revolutionaries who remain humanly acceptable are those who retain this sense of compassion even while engaged in the violence of revolutionary warfare.

I know very well that such moralizing about revolution is "unrealistic," in that the empirical probabilities are against any moral restraints once the tide of violence is released. This, indeed, is the most important reason why one ought to be desperately reluctant to decide upon or to give assent to a course of revolutionary insurrection. I think it is very important and very instructive to understand that the moral logic here is exactly the same as that applying to war. In both cases, the fundamental moral decision that must be made is whether mortal violence can ever be justified. I have deep respect for the pacifist who decides this question in the negative. I cannot share his decision. I believe that in this world there is an obligation to defend the innocent, non-violently if even remotely possible, but with violence if there is no other option. This obligation supersedes the right to suffer martyrdom, at least for most individuals. An individual has the right to choose martyrdom in preference to using violence; I don't concede him the right to impose this choice upon others. For me, as for many of my generation, the confrontation with Nazism has settled this question once and for all. Armed violence against Nazism was not only just but morally necessary, and it was so for the soldier as well as for the resistance fighter. While Nazism represented an evil of monstrous proportions, it was not a unique evil. The moral insights derived from the confrontation with Nazism, therefore, are in principle applicable to other cases.

Along with others I have found that thinking about the war in Vietnam has made me interested in so-called "just war" theories. I have concluded that this war is an unjust war. Unless I'm to become a pacifist, it is logical to ask further what wars, then, might be called just. I see no essential difference between this question and the question about just revolution. In both cases the deepest motive for thinking about questions of justice is the abhorrence of killing. The inescapable moral insight of the Nuremberg trials (whatever else one may think about them) is that duty and patriotism cannot serve as alibis for the crimes of war. The same moral insight applies to revolution. "Wars of national liberation" are no more immune from moral judgment than "wars in the defense of the fatherland." Anyone who wishes to make them so ranges himself against the most significant moral discovery of our time, to wit, that every individual, as an individual, is accountable for his actions.

I don't propose in this essay to set forth a theory of just revolution. I think I have said enough to indicate in what direction my thinking on such a theory would go. But I would like to return for a moment to what I said earlier about sad revolutionaries. There is a whole literature about the tragic grandeur of the profession of arms, some of it indeed romantic and morally reprehensible, but some sharply revealing of the moral ambiguity of violence. I'm thinking, for instance, of De Vigny's *The Military Necessity,* something of a classic of this literature. At its morally most perceptive moments this tradition of military thought has recognized that only those who detest war can be trusted to carry arms and, if need be, to use them. It would be grotesque, in view of the moral fervor that accompanies so much thinking about revolution, if the morality of the revolutionary fell short in this respect of the morality of the soldier. If there is such a thing as a "good soldier" (I think there is), it is an individual with a full sense of the tragedy of violence. The same, I should think, applies to the "good revolutionary." This is why only sad soldiers and sad revolutionaries are to be trusted.

The historical record is not reassuring to those who would lightly embark upon a revolutionary course. I will not discuss the American Revolution in this context. I doubt if it can be correctly described as a revolution in the sense of the previous definition. It was too conservative for that. Certainly the establishment of independence from England was a step of momentous historic import. But as far as my knowledge goes, there was rather little thought of radically altering the social order in the colonies themselves. In the two greatest revolutions of modern history, the French and the Russian, it is very doubtful indeed whether more good than evil came from them for their own time or for subsequent history. The French

Revolution merely hastened a process that was taking place anyway, the coming to power of the bourgeoisie politically as well as economically. It is open to question whether this was such a great thing. But the major unintended consequence of the French Revolution was the growth of nationalism as a major force of modern history, a development that I would look upon as almost wholly unfortunate. At best, the meager fruits of the Revolution in terms of, when all was said and done, a slight extension in political liberties hardly justify the agony of the Terror. As to the Russian Revolution, the present result, in the aftermath of the ocean of blood shed during the Lenin and Stalin periods, seems to be that the average Russian is better off economically and worse off in terms of political liberties than he was in, say, 1910. His greater affluence, of course, is the result of Russia's industrial development in the last thirty years or so. Economists disagree on whether this development was helped or hindered by the Revoluton and its consequences—it certainly was already well under way before the Communists took power. Be this as it may, I see no possible moral calculus that would retroactively justify the nightmares of the 1920s and 1930s in terms of the Soviet gross national product of the 1960s—especially as the life of most Russians before the Revolution was nowhere near to the abject misery that one might take as a just cause for revolt in many underdeveloped countries today.

I'm well aware of the argument that, despite all this, the great cataclysmic events of history produced beneficient change, if only because they changed ideas, values, and consciousness. This argument applies as much to war as it does to revolution. I would not dismiss this line of thinking out of hand, although, particularly as a sociologist, I'm more inclined to look for the roots of lasting change (beneficent or otherwise) in slower, less dramatic processes. But it is true that, in retrospect, we can look upon almost any historical cataclysm and find some good coming from it. The underlying fact here is that all of history is one endless massacre stretching back to the dawn of mankind. Wherever we are in history, we stand on a mountain of corpses—and, however terrible the thought, we are the beneficiaries of all this carnage.

In this perspective it is pointless to moralize about history. It is, however, morally useful to engage in an exercise of the imagination rather similar to the exercise of "contemporaneousness" that Kierkegaard suggested with regard to the New Testament. The exercise is to place ourselves, with our moral perceptions as they are now, into a past historical situation, and to ask, "How would I have stood in this situation?" Such an exercise, needless to say, does not suppose that, if we really had lived as Frenchmen in 1789 or as Russians in 1917, we would then have had the ideas and the values we have today. Of course we would not. The supposition is rather the opposite—namely, that the events of 1789 and 1917 were not so unique that, in altered shape, they could not recur tomorrow. In other words, the exercise is intended to combine the present knowledge of the past and present moral perceptions—for the purpose of providing lessons for future moral judgments.

Again, despite all this, I would reiterate my conviction that there are situations in which revolutions are justified. For example, the Mexican Revolution, another one of the great revolutions of this century, can, I think, be cited as a case in point. The conditions that led to its outbreak were humanly outrageous by any reasonable standard. The consequences, to be sure, have been different from those intended by the revolutionaries, and present-day Mexico can hardly be held up as an ideal society. Nevertheless, it seems that the average Mexican is better off today than he was in 1910, and that this is at least in part directly attributable to the changes brought about by the Revolution.

The purpose of these remarks is not to hand out moral grades to history, and certainly not to map out areas for justifiable revolution in the contemporary world. As to the latter, suffice it to express my conviction that there are areas in the Third World in which revolution now appears as the only alternative to unimaginable human degradation and wretchedness, and that American policies should start as soon as possible to accept this fact. I shall return to this point a little later. But it should also be stressed as strongly as possible that America itself is not one of these areas. *Revolution is not a viable option in America, either practically or morally.*

Revolution in America is a practical impossibility. It seems to me that even those who are so outraged by the ills of American society that they would have no *moral* hesitation in resorting to revolution to cure these ills should be in a position to realize this. Not only is overwhelming power ranged against any would-be revolutionaries, but the overwhelming majority of public opinion as well. The capacity of radical students to create even a ripple of revolutionary upheaval is minimal. The capacity of black militants is somewhat larger. Even they, however, can achieve little more than brief flurries of racial warfare, about the outcome of which there cannot be the slightest doubt. The notion that embroilment in the revolutionary turmoil of the Third World will accentuate the "contradictions" of American society can be plausible only to a mind steeped in the kabbalistic intricacies of Marxist dogmatics. The course of America in the Third World, in the wake of Vietnam, will very probably be in the direction of disengagement, not embroilment—with the probable consequence, incidentally, that such American disengagement will accentuate the "contradictions" in the Third World itself. In any case, what chances of revolution exist in America, however remote, are from the "right" rather than the "left." I would reiterate that I don't consider such a development likely. But it is the only kind of revolution that, given certain circumstances, might have enough power and enough public support on its side to give it a chance of success. Needless to say, this is not the kind of revolution that radical students and intellectuals, white or black, have in mind.

But the idea of revolution in America lacks moral as well as practical plausibility. I think that I'm as aware as anyone on the "left" of the inequities and even the outrages of America. I fully appreciate that there are moments in which one's moral response to these realities takes the form of violent anger. I still find it hard to understand how people, who after all are literate and thus not condemned to a view of the world limited to their own experience, can seriously come to the conclusion that American society is so hopelessly rotten that the anguish and the dubious outcome of revolution are morally preferable to even the *status quo,* let alone to the improvements of the *status quo* that are realistically possible. I don't understand how one can come to such a conclusion either in the perspective of history, or by comparing America with other societies of the present. It is only in comparison with a Utopian future that such a result could conceivably be arrived at, or possibly in comparison with present societies (Cuba, China or what-have-you) that are perceived through the bizarre distortions of Utopian optics. Compared with the Kingdom of God, to be sure, *every* empirical society looks like a mass of perdition. I don't begrudge anyone his Messianic visions, but I refuse him the right to get others killed by his visionary ecstasies. Once one looks at American society with eyes that are freed of Utopian distortions, it appears as a society with remarkable humane achievements. Even more importantly, it appears as a society with a remarkable capacity to reconstruct itself in response to moral challenge and human needs. The irrational rage of the Utopian mentality not only distorts the perception of present reality, but has the probable effect of foreclosing future possibilities, the realization of which requires clear sight and sober action.

It will be amply clear by now that I have little respect for the radicals who brightly talk of a coming American revolution. If they mean it, they are to be condemned. If they don't mean it, they are ridiculous. The one group that I would exempt from this lack of respect are black militants, especially when they are *not* intellectuals. Even if one puts behind oneself the untold oppression of the black past in America, the present situation of blacks in this society is sufficiently oppressive to make understandable revolutionary impulses or acts. Such understanding does not entail moral approval or practical support, but it makes it impossible for me to dismiss the claims of black militancy as I would those of white radicalism. All the same, particularly in addressing oneself to this group, I find it inexcusable, indeed a strange new form of racial paternalism, *not* to challenge the moral and the practical distortions that have been spouted in the name of a putative black revolution. And I have confidence that even those black militants who are too angry to be amenable to moral rebuttal are still open to the rational considerations of practical dissuasion.

But let us return to the white radicals, students, and intellectuals most of them, with whom our consideration of current revolutionary rhetoric began. I really try to be fair. When I hear some pretty coed start talking about the revolution, *I* think of dead Algerian children—I know very well that *she* is thinking of something else, something great and noble and immaculate. I can even, at times, accomplish the feat of listening to a middle-aged professor talk about the revolution and of conceding that, perhaps in some manner invisible to the naked eye, he is being moved by compassion. I'm willing to concede that at least *some* of the revolution talk abroad in America today is the outflow of genuine humanistic impulses. *Most* of it, I'm convinced, is self-indulgence and unseriousness. It is not so much motivated by sympathy with black people in slums and yellow people in rice paddies as by boredom with Connecticut. In this boredom the talk of revolution offers a vicarious identification with adventure, strength and moral purity.

The exact form taken by this identification generally depends on how far the individual has been "radicalized." The fully formed "leftist" identifies with the revolutionary violence directly—that is, as the throats are being slit in the dark of night, he identifies with the killers. The liberal in the process of moving "left" often identifies with the same images in a masochistic mode—*his* identification, pleasurably so, is with the victims. The latter identification is clinically more interesting. It can be observed profitably in what I would call the "Uncle Whitey" complex—the abject submission by white liberals to anti-white invective by blacks. Anyone who has watched such a performance attentively must come to the conclusion that there is libidinal gain in it—for *both* sides. The masochistic logic requires guilt, and if there is no real guilt it must be invented. Only the guilty one is morally justified in enjoying the punishment. We thus have the recurring spectacle of white liberals, whose relations to the black community have been rather more decent than those of most Americans, ritually confessing to the most horrendous sins of "racism." The same psychology can be observed in the moral self-disembowelment practiced by some American liberals abroad. They vie with their accusers in heaping upon themselves every conceivable guilt for American actions in every corner of the world, even actions they had never heard of before. They are sometimes ready to heave upon their broad moral shoulders even the guilt accruing from British or Belgian imperialism—and, in the maximal case, all the wickedness done by white men since history began.

All of this, I'm sure, is of considerable psychiatric interest. Morally, one can say some very simple things. People who are bored in Connecticut will probably be bored anywhere, and in any case they ought to be able to find spiritual energizers that are less dangerous to others who are not bored and have good reasons for wanting to live. People who get vicarious thrills from homicide should seek professional help or watch horror movies. People who want to be whipped should persuade their spouses or lovers to oblige them. As to guilt, the same moral insights that applied to Germans in 1945 apply to all of us today. There is no such thing as collective guilt. Responsibility for what is done by the political community to which one belongs—yes. But not guilt. Not, that is, unless one has participated as an individual, be it by actions or by non-action, in the deeds in question. I'm not guilty of an act performed on the other side of the world by a man wearing an American uniform, even if he pretends to perform it in my name. If that act is evil, then I'm responsible for trying to prevent it or at least for protesting against it, and I become guilty if I don't do these things. But no collective entity—not the nation, not the state, nor a "movement" of any description—can automatically enmesh me in guilt just by virtue of my being assigned membership in it, any more than it can automatically pre-empt my moral choices or grant me plenary dispensation for my immoral acts.

These are really very simple truths, but it seems that they must be repeated in our situation. Imaginary guilt is one of the least likely sources of constructive human action, in politics as in other areas of life. In our situation there has been far too much politics as psychodrama. What we urgently need is people who act politically with sober confidence in their values and their reason, not people who use politics as a substitute for the analyst's couch. We have, God knows, enough social ills to cope with without having to deal at each turn with personal pathology.

I have spoken very harshly of would-be revolutionaries. I think it is necessary to do so. Still, I would reiterate my recognition that, even in Connecticut, there are individuals whose revolution talk comes from motives that I fundamentally cherish. The same recognition, of course, pertains to radicals in general. Very probably every morally viable society requires both "radicals" and "conservatives" —those who impatiently push ahead for necessary changes and those who would apply brakes in the fear that much good may be destroyed along with the bad in the process of change. I have tried to show how a conservative attitude can be rooted in humanistic concern, and I fully recognize that the same concern can underlie a radical stance. Indeed, the whole purpose of this book is to express the belief that conservatives and radicals (and, needless to add, liberals as well) can meaningfully talk to each other on the basis of their common humanistic concern—that, in a word, there is such a thing as a community of the compassionate, cutting across the political and ideological dividing lines. Such conversation, however, requires self-examination and openness on both sides. I believe it requires, on both sides, a liberation from romantic illusions, from blindness to cruelty and from that cult of self-fulfillment that the false morality of popular existentialism has posited as the goal of life. If we begin to meet these requirements, I dare to hope, we may even begin to converse fruitfully about as explosive a topic as that of revolution.

5. On "Issues"

Within the context of "The Movement," it seems to me, the term "issue" is used in at least three senses. First, "issue" means what it means in common parlance—a current problem around which people discuss and take various positions. Second, in the fully "radicalized" circles, "issues" are propagandistic devices, not taken seriously in themselves, around which support can be built and people manipulated. There is also a third current sense of the term, pretty much the opposite of the second. In this sense "issues" are not so much political problems or positions, but dramatic touchstones of personal engagement. "Issues," in other words, are the points of intersection between politics and personal life, between history and biography. The reiterated demand that one "speak to the issues" is thus more than a demand for political relevance. It is also a demand that one define oneself morally in relation to those questions that, at any rate among those asking them, have become touchstones of moral credibility.

I must have said enough here about my general approach to politics to indicate that there are aspects of this moralism that I don't welcome. There is here a strong tendency to divide humanity into the absolutely good and the absolutely evil, in a spirit of both moral arrogance and political simplicity. There is also an "existentialistic" attitude to politics that can be (and today is) a serious threat to sensible and humane approaches to political situations. Indeed, I would take the position that a society is usually in a much happier condition when its politics are *not* touchstones of personal integrity, when politics are considered as part of the ordinary, undramatic routines of life—and when they can be so considered with a good conscience. Nevertheless, I agree that there exist situations in which political questions take on the quality of moral and personal drama, and rightly so. My own relationship to "The Movement" is determined by the fact that I recognize this quality in some of the major questions it is asking. In other words, some of the major "issues" taken as personal touchstones within "The Movement" are just this for me as well. Needless to say, this does not necessarily mean that there is also agreement about the intellectual understanding of these problems or about possible solutions. It does mean that I accept the moral frame of reference within which the problems are perceived— accept it, that is, when this is done out of authentically moral rather than strategic motives.

This further implies that I must recognize the validity of the demand that one "speak to the issues." I shall do so briefly now, in just the sense intended by the demand— that is, not to present an exhaustive analysis or programs of action, but to define myself personally in confrontation with these "issues." There are three that are foremost— Vietnam, black America, and the university.

Issue: Vietnam. It might be useful to say first why I do *not* consider Vietnam a touchstone of moral outrage and engagement. I'm not bothered by Vietnam as a manifestation of American imperial power *per se*. I accept the fact that there are empires in the world, and the American empire, in its performance so far since its emergence at the end of World War II, compares not too unfavorably with most others and very favorably indeed if compared with its current competitors. I'm not morally outraged by the fact that, obviously, American imperial power did not come to Vietnam by invitation of the Vietnamese, though I would prefer it had been that way. American power did not come to central Europe by invitation either, yet its presence there has been, in my opinion, mainly to the good. Nor am I moved to moral excitation by revulsion against the undemocratic character of "our" Vietnamese or by enthusiasm about the political virtues of "theirs." I don't regard western-style democracy as the apex of political perfection, and I'm rather inclined to the view that in a country like Vietnam it is, on the contrary, a political impossibility. As to the regime on the other side of this conflict, it is a bloody tyranny the expansion of which fills me with no enthusiasm whatever.

I *am* morally outraged by Vietnam for very different, and really much simpler, reasons. The Saigon regime is repulsive not because it is undemocratic but because it is murderously oblivious to the welfare of its people. The American presence in Vietnam is morally outrageous not because it is an expression of imperial power but because of the inhuman warfare it has unleashed upon that unfortunate country. The war in Vietnam has been a war against an entire population in a way that no major war fought by the United States has ever been. The inhumanity of this war can be excused by neither the inhuman actions of the other side (no inhumanity ever can), nor by the general statement that *all* wars are inhuman. To be sure, there has been inexcusable cruelty in previous American wars. One need only mention Hiroshima and Dresden. But the peculiar inhumanity of this war lies in its being part and parcel of the basic military strategy of fighting it. That is, the indiscriminate bombing and shelling of civilians, and the devastation of vast areas of the country, are not unfortunate side effects or isolated instances of brutality. They are of the very essence of this war. And so are the policies that have created the masses of wretched refugees, and the practices of terror against prisoners and "suspects" that American forces have collaborated with even if they have left their actual execution to the South Vietnamese. All of this human horror has been summed up in the now-classic statement of an

American officer, "It was necessary to destroy the town in order to save it." The statement applies to the entire American enterprise to "save" Vietnam.

Much of this, I realize, has been the direct consequence of this being a war against insurgency. It is of the very strategy of the insurgents "to swim among the people like fish in the sea," and thus to invite indiscriminate retaliation against the people in order to win their support. America cannot be blamed for this strategy, but it can be blamed for the alacrity with which it responded to the invitation to inhumanity held out by the situation. Nor can America be excused by virtue of its inexperience in this kind of warfare, any more than a rookie policeman can be excused if he shoots indiscriminately into a group of innocent bystanders held as hostages by a criminal. And no amount of inexperience can serve as an alibi for complicity in the torture of helpless prisoners. Morally speaking, if it were really true that all counterinsurgency wars can only be fought as inhumanly as in Vietnam, then this would only be an awesome warning against engaging in such wars—the same moral argument, indeed, that I have used previously in discussing revolutions. I'm also sensible to the observation that this war's cruelties strike us so forcefully because of its instant and intimate coverage by the news media. True, Americans could not watch the bombing of Dresden on television hours after it happened. The immediacy and visibility of the agonies of Vietnam, mainly the result of television, have very probably facilitated a reaction of human outrage. But I have some difficulty seeing this as an argument against the outrage. If television has made it easier for us to feel the pain of people on the other side of the world, this, it seems to me, is a moral argument *for television* and *not* for the actions that inflict the pain.

Personal touchstones have personal stories. I have never been in or even near Vietnam. But I vividly remember a bright summer day a few years ago. I was reading a newspaper in an outdoor cafe in Switzerland, immersed in the sense of orderly well-being which that country is so peculiarly adept in producing and quite at peace with myself. Then my eye fell on a picture in the newspaper. It showed a group of South Vietnamese soldiers torturing a Vietcong prisoner by holding his head under water. I instinctively started to turn the page to get rid of the picture, then stopped myself as I noticed a figure in what looked like an American officer's uniform standing on the edge of the group. It suddenly became important to determine whether it was, in fact, an American. I remember holding the paper close to my eyes, so that I could make out the insignia on the uniform or the racial features of the face. The picture was too blurred. Then I realized that it didn't really matter. I knew that these things were being done and that Americans stood by, both physically (as, possibly, in this instance) and in the sense of complicity. I did not for a moment feel guilty— I was not doing this, I had not been asked, I had not given my assent. But to the extent that all of this was being done in my name, I was responsible for dissociating myself from it. And to the extent that I had any possibilities, however limited, of influencing the course of events, I had an obligation to make use of them. This reaction had nothing to do with ideology or even with politics as such. It was an immediate and irresistible conviction that *this horror must stop*.

I'm not suggesting that my opposition to the American course in Vietnam was produced by this particular incident, or that it was purely emotional and divorced from political reflection. I'm citing the incident because I want to underline the essentially simple impulse, an impulse of outraged humanity, that was the original motive for my opposition. In this, of course, I was not alone. Unlike most radicals of my acquaintance, I'm very rarely certain of my political judgments, and I have over the past years occasionally doubted my judgments about Vietnam. What I *am* certain of is the profound and inevitable rightness of my outrage over this type of inhumanity. I have over and over again come across the same impulse in "The Movement," especially those segments of it that have not yet been ideologized in radical terms, but also among radicals within it. This shared outrage over human suffering makes me able to converse with individuals whose *Weltanschauung* and political positions are drastically different from my own—individuals, that is, whose moral outrages are not restricted to the inhumanities inflicted by those in one particular uniform only.

Vietnam has been the touchstone, for me as for many others, not only for opposition to a specific policy of the American government, but for some intensive reflection about American power in the world generally. It will be clear by now that this reflection has not led me into a "radicalized" stance. I accept American power not only as a fact but, on balance, as a desirable fact. I have no desire to see the disappearance of the American empire, even if this were an imminent possibility, which it is not. What I would like to see is far-reaching changes in American imperial policy, especially in the Third World. These changes are neither very radical nor very original, but have been suggested for a long time by thoughtful observers of different political persuasions: a more prudent employment of military power, more controls over the now still largely unbridled exercise of economic power, a turning away from the ideological view of international affairs as perennial battleground between the good guys of the "free world" and the bad guys of an unchanging Communist conspiracy, and, probably most important of all, a cessation of the policies that have supported any and all regimes as long as they could present themselves as anti-Communist defenders of the *status quo*.

I believe that, precisely in terms of the politics of compassion, it is America's relations with the Third World that will present us with more dramatic moral challenges in the years to come. To meet these challenges, I believe, we will have to question two basic assumptions of the prevailing American view of the world. In the eco-

nomic area, this is the assumption that what is good for
American business is *ipso facto* good for "development."
In the political area, it is the assumption that all revolutionary change is bad (I trust that I've said enough about
revolution to indicate that I did not arrive at this particular
conclusion lightheartedly). If American power in the
Third World will not change its orientations in this direction, then we will be faced with ever deepening failure
before what is likely to emerge as *the* moral challenge
of the coming century or so—the co-existence of unparalleled affluence and unparalleled misery in an era of near-
total communication.

It goes without saying that I'm not persuaded by the
radicals that America is incapable of such change because of the intrinsic nature of its capitalist system. It
seems to me that, on the contrary, it is capitalism rather
than socialism (in any of its empirically available forms
rather than as a Utopian fantasy) that has shown itself
capable not only of producing the economic and technological power that could now transform human life everywhere, but also of fashioning social systems within which
there is political leeway for the humane impulse to do so.
This does not mean a prescription of our sort of capitalism
for the whole world. Indeed, in reversal of the usual
Marxist view of these matters, I'm inclined to think that,
especially in the Third World, some societies will have to
go through a socialist phase in their march toward
capitalism. This is not the place to expound on this.
My point is simply that capitalism is not the root cause
of our misdeeds in the world—no more so, incidentally,
than socialism is that of all the villainies of the Russians.
The history of our entanglement in Vietnam makes this
rather clear. On the other hand, I'm not at all sanguine
about the power centers of America (both the political
and the economic ones) readily changing their previous
imperial policies. There is *a chance* that they will—no
less, no more. But it is, in my opinion, a better chance

than the likelihood of great improvements in the condition of mankind in the wake of a global debacle of American power.

Issue: Black America. Here, once more, I find myself assenting to the moral intensity with which this issue is taken in "The Movement," though I cannot agree with some radical and liberal interpretations of what is involved in the issue. There can be no question in my mind about the validity of positing the question of black America, and of racial oppression generally, in terms of a basic moral dividing line. That is, how an individual responds to the Negro is a touchstone of his human integrity. By and large, I don't think that our time is particularly rich in new moral insights. However, this insight into the human significance of racial attitudes, along with the insight into individual accountability regardless of role, counts among the moral achievements of the age, paid for in tremendous struggle and pain. Any individual who demeans another because of race *ipso facto* depreciates his own humanity. Any society that institutionalizes racial oppression in any form *ipso facto* declares its lack of humanity. These insights, to be sure, are not in themselves new. Their most important historical source, I imagine, is Christianity. What is new in our time is the intensity and the wide popular spread of the ideas of racial equality, both presumably to be attributed to the experience of Nazism. It is this same experience, I think, that has served as the fundamental impetus to the recognition, gaining quite rapidly after World War II, that the worth of American civilization will in large measure depend upon its capacity to right the historic injustice perpetrated against the Negro in its midst.

It is astonishing to me when black militants and radicals today maintain that nothing at all has changed in this situation. The massive collapse of legally instituted segregation in the south, taking place within the short span of a few years, is all by itself a dramatic moral achievement, with far-reaching consequences in the real lives of millions of people. Less visible though in the long run no less important is the simple fact that the abolition of racial inequalities is now officially and publicly on what could be called the agenda of the nation—in terms of government policy, of the behavior of a widening circle of business institutions, and in public opinion at large. Where, indeed, there has been little change (though hardly none at all) is in the economic position of urban Negroes in the North. Tied in as this position is with the problem of poverty generally, and thus with economic structures of considerable complexity, it ought to be clear to any thoughtful observer that this is *not* something that can be solved dramatically by fiats of government. Even this problem, however, is today on the agenda in a way that it has never been before, and the outlook is by no means negative.

To those not blinded by anger or by ideology these facts have been sufficiently clear to create surprise that, now of all times, a revolutionary consciousness should spring up among American Negroes. The historian of revolutions will hardly be surprised. Revolutions typically begin when things are improving, and for humanly very understandable reasons, since hope creates impatience and since only with the coming of realistic hope do oppressed people begin to compare themselves with those in a better position. Both the French and the Russian revolutions are classical cases of this. Thus the revolutionary impulses now coursing through the black communities of America are *not,* as both black and white ideologists maintain, a function of despair. People who are really despairing rarely revolt. Rather, these revolutionary impulses are a function of hope. As such, they are, to a degree, welcome signs. But they are also grave warnings. It would by no means be the first time in human history that impatient anger and ideological illusion have turned hope into despair, and that liberating movements of great promise have ended in ugliness and defeat.

It seems to me that the civil rights movement of the early 1960s was one of the most impressive manifestations of humanity in our time. The current fashion among black and leftist intellectuals to deprecate this movement, and even to mock its martyrs, is as morally deranged as it is factually distortive. I have no doubt in my own mind that the goal of racial integration, in the sense of the full equality and participation of the Negro in American life, was profoundly right morally and politically, and I still hope that it will be vindicated as such by the events of the future. The current notion that it was tried and that it failed is a simple distortion of history. In reality, the trial was just beginning when it was passionately disdained by some of the very people who had been clamoring for it the loudest. The mendacious *volte-face* of many intellectuals on this issue is one of the more repugnant episodes in the political psychology of recent times.

However one may feel about this development, black nationalism is a fact today. In "speaking to the issue" at all, one must address oneself also to this fact. Like most social facts, it is morally ambiguous. While I see some promise in it, I cannot glorify black nationalism in the manner that has now almost become *de rigueur* in the ambience of "The Movement." Nationalism generally is one of the most unfortunate products of the modern west (now, with profound irony, virulent throughout the Third World as an *anti*-western ideology), and I cannot see black nationalism as a shining exception. The fanaticism, the ugly overtones of hatred and violence, and the generation of full-blown mythologies about history—all these, while unfairly ascribed by hostile observers to black nationalism in its entirety, are sufficiently in evidence by now to foreclose the idea that we have here a nationalism greatly different from all others.

On the other hand, I firmly believe that people have the right to define themselves as they see fit. All collective identities are fictitious and arbitrary, and the collective identities we call "nations" appear as naturally given facts only by virtue of habit. "We Frenchmen" is, in principle, no less an imagination than, say, "We Zambians" —there is only more history, and thus more habit, behind the former. What new nationalisms typically posit as the "discovery" of a collective identity is, in fact, an invention, about which there is no necessity whatever. There is no intrinsic, natural or necessary reality to "black identity," any more than to any other collective identity. What is taking place, empirically, is that some American Negroes are inventing themselves as blacks. Still, I would maintain that this is their right. And there is some evidence that the new identity being formed (that is, being *realized*, in the precise sense of *becoming reality*) has some human benefits in terms of self-respect, dignity and a purposeful approach to the real problems of the black community.

Needless to say, I'm troubled by the excesses of the rhetoric and of some of the actions of this new nationalism, not only for themselves but for the potentially dangerous reaction they could provoke from white society. What troubles me most, however, is that these excesses could become highly functional in preventing the very changes that are necessary to improve the situation of black Americans—not only indirectly, by producing a white backlash that will legitimate inaction or worse, but quite directly. I believe that the only viable solution of this problem will lie in a massive program to improve the *economic* position of Negroes in America. Inevitably, this will mean some redistribution of wealth in the society, if only by increasing the tax burdens of the relatively affluent. The things that black nationalists are most urgently demanding, however, have no necessary relation to such an economic restructuring. Recognition of "black consciousness" within the educational establishment, the allocation of black quotas in career systems that were previously merit-oriented, the control of local government machineries by black politicians, and the like—all of these could be instituted (in fact, *are* being instituted) without in any way affecting the economic underprivilege of black America.

To put it brutally, these changes are *cheap*, from the viewpoint of the relatively affluent sectors of American society and, one suspects, from the viewpoint of the power centers in business and government. To put it brutally once more, it could all resolve itself into a proposition of "okay then—let them administer their own slums." There is thus a potential convergence of interests between the most reactionary elements in "the establishment" and the most strident radicals in the black liberation movement. Again, it would not be the first time in history that nationalism has been used in this fashion. I would consider such a development in America as a disaster of the first magnitude and I hope that more black militants will come to be haunted by this prospect.

For "The Movement" as well as for the larger society, the issue of black America has opened up the general issue of poverty in the midst of affluence. It is right that this should be so, right morally as well as right in terms of political reason. In a society as tightly knit by modern communications as ours it becomes intolerable that even a decreasing minority should live in poverty. It is also right that poverty be defined in relative terms—relative, that is, to the life styles of the majority. I have already indicated that I cannot accept the designation of capitalism as the major obstacle in America's capacity to deal humanely with impoverished peoples outside its borders. This applies equally to the problem of poverty within America. Indeed, only the incredible resources created by American capitalism afford an economic base for any attack on the problem that has high promise of success. It goes without saying that such an attack will require a reordering of policies and priorities both in government and in the large economic institutions. The practical urgencies are such that, in this case, I'm far more sanguine about these changes coming about than I would be with regard to changes in

America's relations with the Third World. The current public debate of these matters (including, despite some of its ideological extravagancies, the debate over the place of the "military-industrial complex" in the American economy) is to be taken as a hopeful sign, I think, that the attack on the problem will be more than rhetorical.

Issue: The university. It is on this issue that I have the least sympathy with the positions most common within "The Movement." Indeed, in many ways there is an *ersatz* quality about this issue. The university is a relatively weak and accessible institution. The student rebel, limited in his capacity to initiate revolution in the larger society, acts out a pseudorevolutionary drama on the university campus. The whole thing has frequently reminded me of a man who takes out his resentments against his employer by going home and beating his wife. The university, like the wife, is in a poor condition to defend itself. When, as a result of this, the police are called in, the campus rebel (as the wife-beater in the analogous situation) is full of moral outrage against this invasion of his domestic sphere. The pseudorevolutionary performances on campus are ideologically legitimated by a theory that, *mirabile dictu,* contemporary universities are centers of vast power —a proposition for which empirical evidence is hard to find, but which permits the campus rebel to act in the illusion that a "liberated" university could serve as a *foco* for society-wide revolution. As I have indicated before, all these notions are exercises in false consciousness and their chances of even limited realization are close to nil.

There is, however, a very real crisis of the university, a crisis that has little to do with politics but which, at the moment, is aggravated by the various student movements. The roots of this crisis are, first, the immense increase in the student population, and second, the utilization of the university as a major training and research agency by the large bureaucratic institutions of society. Both developments have undermined the university as a place of exclusive and disinterested scholarship. The second, of course, is much discussed today in terms of the needs of the "military-industrial complex" and other allegedly nefarious interests of the power structure.

To be sure, there is a real issue in the use of the university as, for instance, a place for weapons research. It is important to realize, however, that the basic problem has nothing to do with these particular uses of the university, however reprehensible some of them might be. The use of the university for research on air pollution and for the training of computer engineers (aims that, one may assume, even radicals would be in agreement with) *also* entails the "co-optation" of the university by large bureaucratic structures. What is more, the roots of the university crisis are peculiar neither to America nor to capitalist societies. Socialists, if anything, are even more ambitious in their ideas on mass education and on the utilization of the university for "socially useful" ends. Logically enough, the main features of the university crisis have been remarkably similar in all advanced industrial societies, be they capitalist *or* socialist, with only the significant exception that more vigorous repression has forced the crisis out of public visibility in most of the socialist countries.

What, in my opinion, is happening in the university crisis in America (and to a large extent in western Europe) is that the university is caught between two forces, which at the moment appear as antagonistic, but which may in the rather imminent future be expected to recognize their practical compatibility. These two forces are the youth culture and the large bureaucratic establishments. The youth culture, indeed, is animated by a strongly anti-bureaucratic animus, which at the moment is venting itself against the unfortunate bureaucrats who administer the universities. But as the youth culture progressively wins its battles on the campus (and I have indicated before that this is what, I think, will happen) and thus wins "participation" in the running of academic institutions, the youth culture itself will, inevitably, be bureaucratized.

We already encounter fledgling youth bureaucrats on most American campuses. Their rhetoric is still quite wild (rather like that of labor functionaries in the 1930s), but, with the exception of the out-and-out political radicals, they are already doing mostly what all bureaucrats like to do—attending endless committee meetings, writing endless memoranda, and having lunch with each other and with other bureaucrats. These other bureaucrats, needless to say, are the present university administrators, with whom they share a fundamental hostility to "useless" scholarship and thus an innate suspicion of the faculty. I have complete confidence in the bureaucratization process at work here. Inevitably, as "student power" is institutionalized, it is the bureaucratic types who will occupy the new power positions—others will have better things to do and are unsuitable for this kind of activity anyway. Inevitably, as bureaucrats come to power, they establish convivial relations with other bureaucrats. The end result of this highly predictable development is only inadequately described by the term "co-optation." If anything, the "co-optation" is mutual, as common interests are recognized and rationally organized.

The most likely results of the "student revolution" on the campus itself, then, will be an enlargement of bureaucracy and a further deterioration of the scholarly ideals of the university. The new student bureaucracy, if elected democratically, will represent the majority interests of its constituency. These interests will hardly support scholarly standards or facilitate the disinterested pursuit of knowledge. There is no reason, however, why this type of "liberated" campus should not arrange itself amicably with the larger bureaucratic structures of government and business. Government officials, corporation executives and (last not least) foundation bureaucrats already widely agree that most of what goes on in universities under the heading of scholarship is useless. Their training and research needs can be met either in special programs within the university (the new student bureaucrats can easily be convinced that, say, medical schools still require something as uptight as examinations) or, probably increasingly, in new institutions outside the framework of the universities. Put simply, "the establishment" will be able to meet its own needs without begrudging the youth culture its victory on the campus.

The scenario that emerges from these considerations is fairly simple. Undergraduate colleges, *at least,* will serve as the major institutional locale for the youth culture. They will constitute immense T-groups, bureaucratically administered with inmate participation and programmed to serve the highly elastic needs of the masses of young people being processed through them. "The establishment" will have little difficulty conceding this preserve to the youth culture, and will even be quite willing to subsidize it, since this "restructured" university will not interfere with the "establishment's" own needs and will be popular to boot (*everyone* will get in).

I find this prospect dismaying, partly because it is likely to undermine my own social existence. Once I succeed in abstracting from my personal involvement in this development, I might conclude that society will not be greatly harmed by it. Of course, there are scholars who will become obsolete within the university because of their lack of qualifications to become *either* "honorary youths" within the "liberated" university *or* useful technicians within the bureaucratic R&D establishments, since their interests will be clearly "irrelevant" to both. Such people, however, are not terribly numerous. Most academicians will adapt themselves to the role of "resource persons" to youth as readily as they have already adapted themselves to the requirements of "scientific manpower" of government and business. Some, who knows, might even succeed in accomplishing both accommodations simultaneously. And the hopelessly "irrelevant" academicians, one may surmise, will somehow survive in a society both affluent and tolerant of socially innocuous maladjustment.

I beg to submit, then, that I try to look at the process I perceive here with as much detachment and fairness as my own social position permits. I see the university, as I happen to cherish it, about to be destroyed between the twin "relevances" of the youth culture and the bureaucratic power centers. I will *not* make the mistake of declaring this destruction to be a cosmic disaster. In other words, I will *not* fall into the error of most intellectuals, who habitually regard their own well-being as the most important purpose of social life. What is good for scholarship is not necessarily what is good for a society, and there are more important social purposes than the subsidization of intellectuals. It is too much to ask, however, that I be enthusiastic about what "The Movement" is accomplishing on the university campus. And I'm far too unqualified for the role of "honorary youth" to feel motivated to pretend.

There is, indeed, a kernel of moral validity in the current rebellion against the university. This is the already mentioned demand for the humanization of bureaucracy. I certainly concur in this demand. The bureaucracy of the university, however, is by and large one of the most humane and benign on the American scene already. Thus I find it hard to give this case a very high priority in my own mind.

I would like to repeat that the above discussion of "issues" is *not* intended to provide a detailed discussion of the vast political and social problems they pertain to, *nor* is it supposed to suggest specific programs of political action. Neither is the purpose of this essay. I have taken the issues as they are presented today within "The Movement," not as I would present them in the context of a wider analysis of American society. Also, I have taken the issues seriously as touchstones of personal commitment and I have tried to "speak to the issues" in this sense. In other words, these remarks as well as this essay as a whole are *neither* systematic sociological analysis *nor* a specific political program. Such analytic and programmatic comments as I have made are in the context of personal "alignment" in the face of the current revolutionary upsurge. Put simply, what I have tried to do is to "speak up and be counted" on a number of issues that currently agitate the American scene—not because I feel accountable to all the people who habitually make this demand, but because I would like to be heard by a few among them.

6. On Being an American

Summer 1969: I have been out of the country for two
months. When I come back, there are the flags. Everywhere. Thousands and thousands of them. Stickers with
the flag on cars. Little flags fluttering out of windows,
and some really big ones. On the lawn of a small summer
house on Long Island is an enormous flag hanging on a
flagpole worthy of the commanding general of a full
division.

I like the flags. I like being back in America.

One of my sons picked up a flag sticker somewhere
and has pasted it on the door. A friend comes by and
frowns disapprovingly. "Don't you know what this means?
It means that you're in favor of the war in Vietnam
and that you want to keep the niggers in their place!"
Clearly I'm not in favor of either, and I'm troubled by
the flag sticker on my door. For a moment I feel like
a local secretary of the John Birch Society, or at least the
father of one.

Is this what the flags mean? Is my friend right? I'm
not sure. In part he is probably right. There is a high
correlation between the flags and such noble sentiments,
also spouted on car stickers, as "Register Communists, not
guns" and (beginning to look a little scratchy now) "Wal-
lace in '68." I suspect that there is more to it than that,
though. There is a whole wave of class resentment and
assertion, with working-class and lower-middle-class whites
wanting to affirm loudly that they too are around, and
that they still believe in the old values of patriotism, hard

work and washing behind the ears. But there is still more, I think. I don't know whether one ought to hang flags out of the window. I do know that one must not permit the John Birch Society and its ilk to pre-empt American patriotism. Indeed, there is a political mandate of preventing such pre-emption.

There are different modes of being an American. Image: A fat, red-faced man, preferably with a cigar sticking out of his mouth, growling threateningly: "If you don't like it here, why don't you go back where you came from?" No, thank you. Image: A chorus of unisexed youths emitting, from out of a luxurious penumbra of hair, the ritual chant: "Shame, guilt; shame, guilt; shame, guilt." No, thank you, too. There are other ways of being an American.

America today generates images of all sorts. Two men stepping onto the surface of the moon. Endless miles of car cemeteries. Machines of such complexity that they seem to come from another world. Packed highways, littered landscapes, polluted air. The faces of men in laboratories, out of which, in our generation, may come the conquest of cancer. The faces of men in the War Room of the Pentagon. The face of Robert Frost. The face of Mayor Daley. The most awesome explosion of human intelligence and human skill in the history of man. The streets of Bedford-Stuyvesant. Endless miles of art galleries, the best in the world. The seemingly perennial scene of troops landing on some godforsaken beach. One recoils from the images of America and one is irresistibly drawn to them. Not only if one is American. The images of America are watched by the whole world.

This summer an acquaintance of mine went to an Indian festival in Oaxaca, in Mexico. There were thousands of people, Indians and tourists. It so happened that the festival began on the day that Apollo 11 landed on the moon. Television sets had been set up on the main plaza. There was some desultory Indian dancing going on at the edge of the plaza, but only some tourists were watching it. The Indians sat transfixed before the television sets. The real festival was the American one, staged on the moon.

Individuals love their country for various reasons. Most of the reasons have nothing to do with politics. And I'm sure there are differences between those who were born and spent their childhood in a country and those who, like myself, came to this country as adults. There are different webs of loyalties, memories, associations. Often these are clearly recognized only abroad, in the experience of missing one's country. Such as the vastness of space in America, physical as well as social space. Such as the peculiar richness of the American language. Such as specific American sights. The cool elegance of Park Avenue on a winter evening, just after it has snowed. The lonely awareness of a Midwestern bus depot in the small hours of the night. The startling finality of the Pacific, seen from a mountain. All these, of course, are highly subjective. But, whatever one's images of America, there ought to be the rational recognition that the decisions made here today and in the foreseeable future are the decisions that, more than any others, will shape the future. America, in a terrifying sense indeed, is where the action is. And to be an American is, like it or not, to be at the center of action.

Vastness in scale has always been a crucial trait of America. Both the promise and the ugliness of America today are vast. Very different things are going on in America simultaneously—and vastly. The vastness of our imperial misadventures. Vast inhumanities, self-righteousness, and folly. At the same time, a vast upsurge of a new human sensitivity. Take just one example. 1968: a year of ferocious war and civil strife. The year of the assassinations in Memphis and Los Angeles. The year of the Chicago convention. This same year 1968 was the first year in the history of the United States in which there was no legal execution. And hardly anyone noticed this staggering fact. The human promise and the human menace of America are growing side by side. The power to transform the world and the power to blow it up. The readiness, among different individuals, to do either. It seems to me that American patriotism today means, above all, to participate in this drama, personally and also politically.

As a sociologist, I'm professionally attached to an intrinsically debunking perspective on society. I have once called this perspective a precarious vision. It is precarious because it understands the fictions, the arbitrariness and the transitoriness of human institutions. No institution and no society can claim sacredness, necessity or eternal validity for itself. American society and its institutions are no exception to this. Yet (to use a phrase from theology) "in, with, and under" the institutional forms there may be found human values and human achievements of great worth. It seems to me that the precarious vision of society must also include a sense of the precariousness of these values and achievements, especially in a period of rapid and inevitable change. In America today this means *both* a readiness for the changes that ought to come about *and* the will to preserve the valid human accomplishments of the American experience. There are many of these. Not the least of them is the moral outrage and the upsurge of a new humanistic awareness that has marked "The Movement" in the last few years, a phenomenon with unmistakably American accents.

The participation in the American drama I have in mind is that of free individuals. Freedom means to refuse absorption by "systems." Freedom also means a refusal to be "co-opted" by any horde. Such freedom can place one in difficult situations, marginal to all organized groups, sometimes reviled by all of them. Yet there are many individuals in America today who are free in this sense, as there are many, in nearly all political camps, who belong to what earlier I called the community of the compassionate. One of the more breathtaking possibilities on the contemporary American scene is that these individuals may discover each other and make that discovery politically relevant.

THE THOROUGH
REVOLUTIONARY

RICHARD JOHN NEUHAUS

1. The Movement

It is a mass movement of revulsion against mindless slaughter in Vietnam. It is an elitist movement of political *illuminati* who refine the theories of class warfare. It is a black movement of isolation to build identity and resources for blackness in power rather than dependence. It is a black movement of alliance with any color or nationality prepared to join in overthrowing capitalist imperialism. It is a black movement of militant faith that the promise of the American Experiment can be invoked for the liberation of black and white alike. It is a youth movement in search of community and personal meaning beyond consumption and technology. It is a youth movement in resistance to hypocrisy and fear, to the gift of a poisoned heritage which they did not ask for and do not want. It is also a middle-aged movement of discarded dreams retrieved. It is, far from simply, the Movement.

Although many presume to try, no one can speak for the Movement. There are many voices in the Movement. Some celebrate the splendor of its diversity, the Bastille of the Great American Way has been stormed and the prisoners freed to do their thing. Others talk about the notorious fragmentation of the Left, either because they are frustrated in their efforts to capture the Movement for their program or because they hope the Movement will dissolve and allow a return to business as usual. But for all its fragmentation or diversity, as the case may be, the Movement is. And it will likely be with us beyond the foreseeable future. Although its perpetually changing style should prevent anyone's getting used to it, it is worthwhile to try and understand it.

The Movement resists definition but not description. For fear that they find themselves again trapped in some category of social opinion or posture, some participants urge that we not talk about the Movement at all but just let it "happen." This is a winsome suggestion but quite impracticable for those of us who are dependent upon language, especially in the writing of books. To be sure, no description can be definitive, yet it must be adequate enough to differentiate the Movement from the organizations, attitudes, and even other movements in American life. One characteristic of the Movement, for instance, is that anyone who ventures to describe a characteristic of the Movement can count on being refuted from within the Movement. While the Movement is not an organization, and certainly not a membership organization, there are those within it who issue membership cards. There are also offices of the Holy Inquisition that do not shrink from promulgating anathemas against forbidden ideas and excommunications of apostates. And if the condemnations are sometimes mutual, with many bewildered souls caught in the crossfire, this too is part of the aforementioned splendid diversity in the Movement.

Why then should one want to identify with a phenomenon so amorphous and fractious? My answer is that the Movement is the most hopeful among the forces reshaping American life. The Movement, as discussed in this context, is the totality of movements mentioned in the first paragraph above. *The Movement is the cluster of persons, organizations, world views and activities located on what is conventionally called the Left and acting in radical judgment upon the prevailing patterns, political, economic, social, and moral, of American life.* While there are elements of the genuinely new, the Movement is not without antecedents or correlates in other times and other places. Its members are suspicious of institutionalization, but the Movement has its organizations and bureaucracies. There is resistance to the imposed and programmatic, but the Movement has its organized activities and forms of ritual behavior. There is defiance toward inhibiting orthodoxies, but the Movement has its doctrines and even its dogmas.

Critics of the Movement find cause for ridicule in what they see as its self-contradictory character. In fact these conflicting dynamics demonstrate merely that the Movement has not escaped the human condition. Its institutional, programmatic, and intellectual forms bear witness to the determination to do something about the human condition. It is possible to be in or out of the Movement, which is the most elementary requirement of any social grouping. "We know who the 'we' is and we know who the 'they' is," declared one girl after a lengthy group discussion of the Movement's self-definition. To be part of the Movement does not require being an honorary black (if you are white) or, to use Berger's term, an honorary youth (if you are over thirty), although there are some who promote these admission requirements. One is part of the Movement if he participates in the life of the Movement.

The Life of the Movement

Participating in the life of the Movement means sharing in the activities, ideas and, to a lesser extent, the organizations associated with the Movement. Eric Hoffer, author of *The True Believer* and the power elite's professional common man, would be quick to point out the similarity to a religious movement. The Movement has its church (organization), doctrine (ideas) and ritual (corporate cultic activities, complete with vestments). He might go on to say that the Movement is the creation of society's misfits and weaklings who have a desperate need to "belong" in order to compensate for their unconscious self-loathing. All of which is as fascinating as it is misleading. The pathology so scathingly described by Hoffer is no doubt present in every movement. Published in 1951, *The True Believer* was applauded by the liberal elite as an indictment of the movement surrounding the first McCarthy. Today the same liberals, now "radicalized" and self-consciously part of the Movement, find themselves the subjects of Hoffer's unflattering diagnosis. Hoffer was wrong then and he is wrong now. (I mention Hoffer in particular because, to give the devil his due, *The True Believer* is probably the most effective popular polemic against mass movements in recent American writing. Those who are unfamiliar with it should not settle for this discussion of it but submit themselves to Hoffer's full, cruel, and sometimes healingly accurate analysis.)

Eric Hoffer and others who presume to remain aloof from movements, preserving their uncompromised autonomy and dispassionate objectivity, reveal a self-deceptive arrogance. Arrogance, because there is an implied superiority to "the great unwashed" who respond to humanity's itch for fulfillment through radical change. Self-deceptive, because the presumably aloof become in fact the unwitting agents and victims of the decisions of others, whether these be the forces of establishment or insurgency. Paraphrasing Jesus, he who would preserve his autonomy loses his autonomy.

This does not mean that everyone outside the Movement is guilty of self-deceptive arrogance. A person may participate in other movements counter to the Movement. This is an error of judgment, I believe, but not necessarily an instance of moral default. Another person may have such a fragile hold upon his identity that he dare not make himself vulnerable to the critical exchange that marks a lively movement. Yet another may have come to the profoundly pessimistic conclusion that no movement holds realistic hope for change for the better. No doubt there are others with other reasons. Peter Berger, for example.

Those who are in the Movement are in it, one hopes, because they recognize that if change is to be effected it must be done through corporate action. They know that a group, any group, modifies and makes ambiguous the clarity of individual intention. They understand the perversions attached to the term "mass movement" but they also know that, for the most part, a mass movement is only a small movement that has grown big. Every movement runs the risk of becoming monolithic, intolerant, and an enemy of the freedom it professes to seek. The Christian movement of Dostoevsky's Grand Inquisitor no longer had any room for the restless ways of its Founder. The Movement under discussion here is no more immune to distortion. The answer to dehumanizing movements is not no movement but humanizing movements. As we shall see, there are dehumanizing elements and sectors within the Movement. Unchecked they could conceivably destroy the Movement's potential for creative change. It is certain, however, that they will not be checked by criticism from outside the Movement but only by those who take the risks of involvement by committing themselves to what is worthy in the Movement.

Where the Movement Has Been

The Movement is usually dated from the early sixties. The formation of the Students for a Democratic Society at Ann Arbor and the issuance of the Port Huron Statement contributed to American political discussion terms such as New Left and participatory democracy. But many of the Movement's roots are discovered in the civil rights thrust of the late fifties. Its early style and tactics were inseparable from the freedom rides and sit-ins, the whole beautifully innocent aggregate of activities that built a context of plausibility for Martin Luther King's argument for the force of righteousness in social change. This is the Movement of liberal nostalgia, which reached the apex of its first phase in Selma, 1965. At a Chicago meeting of the McCarthy-oriented Coalition for a Democratic Alternative shortly after the assassination of Senator Robert Kennedy, a young Kennedy worker declared, "Those of you who did not love Senator Kennedy and believe in his promise cannot begin to understand how we feel, and I would only sound foolish and maudlin if I tried to explain that." In the same way we can empathize with liberals who must restrain themselves to keep from talking about the Movement's earlier days.

But more than empathy is required. Those who came to political consciousness after 1965 need to understand the liberal's remembrance of things past. It is not all nostalgia, naïveté, and spineless sentiment. If the confident "I have a dream" of the 1963 March on Washington has not been vindicated by subsequent events, the dream is no less touched by nobility. If today we deem ourselves more sophisticated and hard-nosed in analyzing the radical changes American society requires, it does not detract from the courage and vision of an earlier struggle whose failure revealed the mastery of racism and brutality in American life. The Movement today is weaker if it forgets Herbert Lee, Medgar Evers, Andrew Goodman, Michael Schwerner, James Chaney, Jimmy Lee Jackson, and the host of others whose devotion was sealed with martyr blood. The Movement is weakened by fledgling radicals who try to exhibit their virility by scorning the civil rights movement as a faint and futile exercise in wishful thinking. The test of manhood is still to be, in the words of Che Guevara, "one of those who risks his skin to prove his truths." We can speak of the Movement pre-1965 without embarrassment or condescension.

We have not outgrown but must still aspire to Martin Luther King's dream of 1963. To be sure, ours is a different and more sobering estimation of what ails America. But it is a smug delusion to think we have arrived at the *kairos,* the appointed moment, in which all the mysteries of history are manifest. In the spring of 1968, during the revolt at the City College of New York, a radical student activist, weighted by a depressing discovery, asked me, "Have you ever thought that maybe there isn't going to be a revolution to change everything, that maybe history will show that what we've been doing is just part of a long reformist tradition?" It is a crucial question for every would-be revolutionary. One can refuse to contend with the question and seek refuge in the security of the dizzying rhetoric of revolutionary cadres. Or, in more manly fashion, he can come off his high, evaluate the unlikelihood of his uniqueness, and then dare to take his chances with history's judgment. If he chooses the second course, with the courageous modesty it requires, he will not feel superior to the Movement pre-1965, but will try to be worthy of its company.

Analysis and Action

Emphasis on the Movement's continuity must be balanced by those elements which seem new and discontinuous. I will not attempt here to even sketch the particulars of the development of the New Left, the emergence of Black Power consciousness, the widespread practice of confrontation politics, and similar factors shaping today's Movement. It is more to the point to examine some of the ingredients of the rationale which informs the over-all phenomenon we call the Movement. After 1965, radical political analysis became a more prominent feature in the Movement. This is reflected in one radical's statement in late 1969. A community organizer, he pronounced himself unimpressed by the action of a group that had raided a New York draft board and destroyed files. "We're past the time of being distracted by radical actions. I don't care how radical somebody acts, what I want to know is what kind of analysis he has." Most radicals acknowledge a greater interdependence between theory and action, but this organizer's emphasis on "analysis" has become typical of large sectors within the Movement. Efforts to resolve problems, correct injustices, or protest outrages are not enough. The insistence now is that all these problems are symptomatic of a more fundamental corruption—call it capitalism, call it imperialism, call it racism, call it liberal democracy, call it consumer enslavement, call it the arrogance of power, or call it everything at once. The point is that the evil is inherent in, and not accidental to, the American Way. The offense against humanity is by habit and not by exception. Not this or that malfunction (which, in radical analysis, is not a *mal*function but a too perfect functioning) must be remedied, but The System Itself must be changed. This is the distinctive dogma of the Movement.

It is a dogma in the pejorative sense of the term. It is authoritatively promulgated, acceptance is required for belonging, it is the definitive referent for the development of further theory and action. But it is also dogma in a more neutral sense, as the identifying rationale of a social grouping called the Movement. To date no person or group within the Movement has been able to become the voice that definitively spells out the dogma's implications. "The System Itself must be radically changed" is affirmed by devotees of flower power and gunpowder alike; it is preached at the pulpits of prestigious churches by black men demanding reparations and in the pulpits of student revolutionary caucuses. It infiltrates itself into the literature of organizations founded for liberal uplift and, with different intonations, is the rallying cry for rushing the police lines in asserting "community control" of Berkeley's parks and Brooklyn's public schools.

A notion that means so many different things to different people, it might be suggested, means nothing at all. But surely it means something when hundreds of thousands of a country's citizens claim to believe that the existing political and economic order is not only incapable of resolving the country's problems but is instrumental in perpetuating them. I suspect a majority of the nation's college students would find nothing debatable in Dr. King's statement of April 4, 1967, "America is the greatest purveyor of violence in the world today." Nor would they be inclined to contest his further analysis that American violence is overwhelmingly on the side of oppression against needed revolutionary change in the Third World. In short, the central insight of the Movement is so deeply planted in contemporary American consciousness that it cannot be treated as a passing phenomenon. The widespread acceptance of this central insight or dogma, the large domain of a radical mood in the country, is what the more explicitly revolutionary in the Movement see as the essential "conditioning" of the public mind which constitutes a classically pre-revolutionary situation in America. Such reasoning assumes, as is endlessly reiterated, that it takes only a committed three per cent of the population to make a revolution.

One can anticipate several ways in which the influence of the Movement may be stemmed. Liberals and rightists alike are aware of the potential of repression which can lead to a fascism American style. Many in and out of the Movement fear that the Left's tendency toward fragmentation is inexorable and they do not need to search far to find the evidences of factionalism. If these increase the Movement could neutralize itself by exhausting its energies in internecine warfare. These and other developments which could abort the promise of the Movement should be taken seriously. There is no room for a mystical euphoria that assumes the Movement, as its name suggests, must inevitably move forward from battle to battle, bloodied but unbowed, on to final triumph. The revolutionaries among us should remember that Marx himself understood that "historical necessity" does not guarantee a set of inevitabilities to meet every contingency successfully. At the same time, there is every reason to hope that the insurgency that has grown in recent years will gain in confidence and strength and will indeed radically change the System.

I believe the critics who attribute the Movement solely to the Vietnam war and assert that it will decline, if not disappear, upon the ending of that conflict are mistaken. It is true that the Movement in recent years is inextricably linked to Vietnam. The war was the organizing focus, the inescapable horror that compelled liberals to re-examine their loyalties and forced the nonpolitical out of their lethargy. No doubt, when this war is over, many who protested will return to the anonymity of public opinion polls. Some of them will credit the American Way for its ending the war, and others, incapable of accepting the idea of American military defeat, will blame the very protest in which they shared. But these are not the people who, by even the most generous definition, comprise the Movement.

New and Old

The Movement is composed of the young who came to political consciousness during the debate about Vietnam. For them, the war was neither tragic error nor fall from grace, but simply what America is all about. Their elders began with an American Dream and felt their faith betrayed by the war. The young begin with the war and are incredulous that someone could feel betrayed by this America. The Movement is comprised also of liberals, frequently and with foolish embarrassment trying to hide their liberal pasts, who have been compelled to the conclusions of radical youth. Their arrival is by a more circuitous and painful route, often being forced to throw off ideological baggage and sometimes coerced to trample ritually upon values they had proudly displayed on the banners of a thousand good causes. Value-free research, the two-party system, the appeal to public conscience, the power of rational discourse in resolving conflict, reliance upon the courts for the redress of grievances, establishment responsiveness to an informed electorate—the road to radicality is littered with such discarded baggage.

The over-thirty converts have come to the Movement naked in the hope of being accepted as honorary youth. If remnants of their liberalism are exposed, they are, like all new converts, fervent in their confession and grateful for absolution. They become masters of one-Leftmanship, ever prepared to go one step further to demonstrate they really belong in the community of the saved. There is an undeniable pathos about this sector of the Movement.

Less pathetic non-youth elements, often dismissed as the Old Left, are evident enough in the councils and projects of the New. For years they took refuge in radical debating societies where they argued the relative merits of syndicalism, anarchism, communism, and the revisionist modifications of each. There are a few old Wobblies, a handful of the staunchest Communist Party faithful who did not lose their faith during the period of the Soviet Union's brutal purges and collusion with Hitler's Germany. "We're used to being an embattled minority," one Communist Party veteran told me, "and I'm not taken in by this radical movement today that's riding a popular tide. You don't know yet whether it has any revolutionary potential." Meanwhile, the most committed people from the Old Left will strategically identify with the New. They, like some critics in the American establishments, are counting on repression sooner or later, but hope it will be later, after the Movement has grown enough, in numbers and ideology, that repression will force an alliance that will bring together the serious revolutionaries.

Others among the Old Left have only disdain for the Movement. Either they have abandoned the ideology of class warfare and hope for socialism through the political process, or they are distressed by the ideological immaturity of the more fervent radicals in the Movement. A veteran of the Workers' Party of America who earned his stripes during the 1920s and now lives quietly in Brooklyn Heights has not given up on the Marxist eschatology. But he too is doubtful about the present Movement. "Listen to some of these kids! They think they invented the idea of revolution. They read a middle-class professor's primer on Marxism and think that makes them theoreticians. It's like confusing comic books with Shakespeare." The pique is understandable and is no doubt shared by thousands who sincerely believed in "the god that failed" and perhaps secretly hope that the report of his death is much exaggerated.

The fact that many of the Old Left identify with the Movement should be no embarrassment. While they are no doubt interested in capturing the enterprise, so are others, and each must be resisted. Any capturing will be done only if the larger society strikes against the Movement in relentless repression and forces retrenchment. In that case all bets are off, but it seems likely that the severely reduced Movement would gravitate toward the best organized institutional base. On those terms, the Old Left does not have much competition. Meanwhile, however, the Old Left's personnel, organizing ability, and money can be welcomed.

It may sound strange to talk about the money of the Old Left, since everyone knows that the Communist Party, for example, has never emerged from the economic depression. Nevertheless, a sizable amount of the Movement's funding comes from people who see black liberation and anti-war activities in continuity with their Old Left commitments. The chief executive of a company involved in New York's shipping industry is one of the main contributors to what is generally considered a "moderate" peace organization. In the early thirties he was a member of the Communist Party and still privately describes himself as "a communist by commitment." He explains his support: "1939 and then the suppression of the International [Communist International dissolved in 1943] killed any real chances for communism as such here. McCarthy [Joseph] was just a late confirmation of the fact. But you can't kill the ideas. I don't think we're going to live to see a revolution, but we can get a hell of a lot closer to the kind of country we wanted when we were active in the Party. Right now I'd give my money to Gus Hall [American Communist Party leader] if I thought it'd do any good. But that isn't where the ideas are. So I kick in to [name of peace organization]."* He "kicks in" generously.

No one should be surprised if rightist groups use the above remarks as an "admission of guilt" that organizations on the Left are fronts of a communist conspiracy. One of the refreshing contributions of the Movement is to help create a greater candor in American political discussion. When the established churches, from the Vatican to the Southern Baptists, endorse Christian-Marxist dialogues, and the President of the United States asks that negotiation replace confrontation between the two imperial powers, it should not be too controversial if movements for social change acknowledge their points of agreement and alliance with the Old Left. As early as 1966 groups like the National Mobilization to End the War in Vietnam insisted on being "nonexclusionary." That is, they rejected the restriction that most liberal organizations imposed on themselves in the early fifties, excluding members of the Communist Party. In 1967 the National Committee for a Sane Nuclear Policy (SANE) dropped the following: "Therefore members of the Communist Party, or individ-

* The name of the organization is withheld in deference to its sensitivities, healthy or otherwise, about accepting "tainted" money. Needless to say, many organizations in the Movement define "tainted" differently, meaning funds from the CIA or other government sources.

uals who are not free because of party discipline or
political allegiance to apply to the policies of the Soviet
or Chinese governments the same standards by which they
challenge others, are barred from any voice in deciding
the Committee's policies or programs."

The Old Left, then, is part of the Movement. It is a
small part, far from being in a position of control or
even major influence, but it has some seasoned warriors,
some affluent friends, an ideological armory, and the patience to wait for repression or other discouragement to
force the Movement in its direction. The Old Left is
very good at waiting.

Black Liberation

In addition to the youth, the honorary youth, and the Old
Left, the Movement is related to black liberation. There
is a symbiotic relationship, undeniable although often
denied, between white and black radicalism, including the
most rigorously separatist versions of the latter. At the
beginning of the 1970s it is clear that there are three
chief, and mutually exclusive, thrusts of militant black
activism: (1) Strategic and/or ideological isolation, sometimes called separatism; (2) A black-led redemption of
the social experiment for all Americans; (3) Revolutionary
alliance. Elements of each thrust are evident in most black
organizations and each of the three groupings has several
sub-groupings. In the first, separatist, grouping is the movement toward "black capitalism." Ideological separatism is
better represented by the variety of black nationalist
groups, some of a religious character, that envision a
separate state or a movement to Africa. The second
grouping, aimed at making the American experiment work
for blacks (and, not so incidentally, changing the way
it works for whites by ending racism) is unambiguously

represented by NAACP, Urban League, and, in a style more congenial to the Movement, by Southern Christian Leadership Conference. The third grouping of revolutionary alliance is most clearly manifest in the Black Panthers and in the writings of its chief ideologist, Eldridge Cleaver.

Some of the black organizations, or so it seems, can in no sense be considered part of the Movement. The black capitalists have difficulty in refuting the charge that they are the Establishment's boys. "Wanting a piece of the economic action" is a goal that can be, and has been, endorsed also by President Nixon and hardly constitutes a "judgment upon the prevailing patterns, political, economic, social and moral, of American life." Organizations such as the Urban League can theoretically aim at major, even radical, change in American life, but are in style and strategy too tied to the prevailing power interests to be considered part of the Movement. The same is true of the NAACP, at least in the North, but probably not in the deep South.

The two groups that seem in some respects to be farthest apart are the two that are most clearly involved in the Movement, the Southern Christian Leadership Conference and the Black Panthers. The first is committed to militant non-violence and the second to class conflict and revolution. Each is emphatically black in leadership and consciousness, but both reject isolation. They agree the essential conflict is not defined by skin color but by the line between exploited and exploiter, haves and have-nots, rich and poor. In dramatically different ways, each works for a black liberation that will result in a liberation for the whole society and, implicitly, for the oppressed of the world. These two organizations and others like them most warrant our attention. Black isolation can go its way with the endorsement of the conservative Republican Party and the liberal Ford Foundation. Isolationist separatism, the masters of the American Way well know, is the cheap solution to "the colored problem." If it is capitalist separatism, it cannot help but strengthen the

System. (In fact this is really integration with white America at its most debilitating point, American big business.) Nationalist separatism cannot really hurt anyone but other black people. While isolationist talk has often seemed to whites to be the most strident and belligerent of black rhetorics, it is also the most harmless. Its chief injury is to the psyches of whites who are made to feel unwanted or denied the satisfaction of sharing vicariously in the black mystique.

Black isolationism agrees with the Movement's negative judgment upon American life. Indeed the judgment is so harsh as to require the equivalent of Jahweh's admonition to the children of Israel regarding the tribes that surrounded them, "Come out from among them lest ye share in their uncleanness." But isolation can do nothing to change America except deprive it of its black population. And, although America exploits its black people while it has them, the dangerous fact is that few of the enterprises that matter to most Americans would be crippled by the absence of black people.

A few years ago an off-Broadway play, "Day of Absence," showed a southern town waking up one morning to discover all its black people gone. The whole town came to a grinding halt, so dependent were the whites upon their niggers. Fortunately, the United States of America is not Dothan, Alabama. At the same time, nothing so clearly demonstrates the calculated cruelty of American racism than that, after three hundred years of using the black man, white America is confident that the black man is expendable. Germany, to suggest an unpleasant but inevitable comparison, was in 1930 many times more dependent upon the Jews than is white America upon the black man. Dependence here has to do with the numbers and influence of Jews in business, finance, the sciences and the arts, compared with the same factors regarding blacks in American society.

I feel it necessary to have dwelt at some length on black isolationism because, I believe, it has inordinately preoccupied the Movement. White radicals have been too eager to support separatist-isolationist demands, with their apparent militancy, and have thus inadvertently strengthened the most odious of racist responses to the future of the black man's role in American life. In a 1968 meeting in New York on radical politics, a small group of blacks decided to hold a caucus apart from the larger meeting. The whites at first resisted, urging that all decisions be made openly and in the full assembly, until a white woman in exasperation shouted out, "Let 'em go! Who needs 'em anyway?" It was a slip of the tongue, of course.

In North Carolina a black speaker was holding forth with impassioned eloquence. Sitting beside me at the rally was a white man who had worked hard for racial justice over the years but had recently been excluded from a previously interracial organization. The speaker reached his climax, as it were, with a vehement "Listen, white man! There's only one thing we want you to do! Like we said to Pharaoh, we say to you, 'Let my people go!'" With a tired smile the white man mumbled, barely audible over the applause, "OK, man, go. Just go away and leave us alone." Black men, with good reason, often express the suspicion that even the most trustworthy white allies keep the word "nigger" in reserve and will some day let it slip. A yet more serious worry is the white man's suppressed wish, "Just go away." In this century of technologically efficient genocide nobody should have to be reminded that such wishes can be realized.

There is a double edge to white support, whether radical or conservative, for black isolationism. Whether the whites speak of black capitalism or black revolutionary solidarity, something else is heard by those who have ears to hear: Let them go! Who needs them? It is probably more true in 1970 than it was in 1940 that, in the words of Gunnar Myrdal's *An American Dilemma:* "If we forget about the means for the moment, and consider only the quantitive goal for Negro population policy, there is no doubt that the overwhelming majority of white Americans desire that there be as few Negroes as possible in America or [that they be] greatly decreased in numbers."

Tactical withdrawal should not be confused with isolation. By now it is a commonplace that black participation in social change must be black-led, that blacks insist upon being the artisans of their own destiny. The power of decision-making for the black role in radical action must be uncompromisingly black. This insistence is not based so much on black nationalist ideology as it is on the black experience of white betrayal. The isolationist path is the easy way to maintaining black autonomy. The more difficult and radical course is being charted by black leadership involved in strategic alliance and conflict with the dynamics of change in the whole society.

It is a mistake for whites to think that "tactical withdrawal" is only a sign of black disillusionment with black-white co-operation or a reflection of black weakness in search of identity. Such withdrawal is pre-eminently a sign of growing black strength and self-confidence. An impotent people incapable of leadership dare not let go of its fragile hold on majority "reality." Only a people who have already discovered their own potential for power and pride can withdraw to solidify and nurture that potential. The isolationists use the more abrasive language about despairing of white America, but their escape to marginal existence suggests they in fact despair of their power to cope with the enormous forces of American oppression.

The Black Mission

For those who care about radical change, the significant black is the black who will not leave white America alone. Dr. King spoke about the black man's "mission" to "redeem all of America." One black Michigan college student protested, "I'm not busting my black ass to save the white man's soul or his way of life. He can save his own soul, if he has one." The protest is against the militant's caricature of Dr. King's position, that the black man is the sacramental agent of redemptive suffering and should passively die that others may live. This is one of the central theses refuted by Stokely Carmichael and Charles Hamilton in their influential *Black Power* and has subsequently become part of the common coin in black rhetoric. Every revolutionary movement has some notion of redemptive suffering. Some must die if mankind is to be liberated in a new order. The black point, however, is that the suffering and dying should be more equitably distributed.

The black man does have a peculiar historical mission. This is clear in the strategy and pronouncements of groups such as the Black Panther Party and SCLC. The "Manifesto" presented by James Forman and adopted by the National Black Economic Development Conference in Detroit, April 1969, is unequivocal: "Black people in this country must understand that we are the Vanguard Force. We shall liberate all the people in the U.S. and we will be instrumental in the liberation of colored people the world around." With evident reference to groups that would isolate black influence in separatist programs, the Manifesto urges that blacks not be "trapped into diversionary and reactionary movements."

In explaining the vanguard mission of blacks, the Manifesto falls into chauvinism: "All the parties on the left who consider themselves revolutionary will say that blacks are the Vanguard, but we are saying that not only are we the Vanguard, but we must assume leadership, total control, and we must exercise the humanity which is inherent in us. We are the most humane people within the U.S." In a more sober vein, the Manifesto puts the black revolutionary mission on the politically solid reasoning that blacks recognize themselves as "the most oppressed group of people inside the United States." They best know the subtle and deadly ways of American exploitation.

In the view of many blacks, the only two ways open are isolation or revolution. In the 1967 Black Power Conference in Newark this resolution was approved: "Be it resolved that the Black Power Conference initiate a national dialogue on the desirability of partitioning the U.S. into two separate and independent nations, one to be a homeland for white and the other to be a homeland for black Americans." Commenting on the resolution, Robert S. Browne, a prominent participant in the conference, writes, "All of those who applauded and approved the resolution can by no stretch of the imagination be considered active partisans of the idea of a separate state. But just as surely as black people have become progressively more disillusioned at the prospect of ever finding a dignified niche for themselves in American society, so have they become more eager to explore any avenue which may offer greater promise."

In the Movement today there is a growing confidence that blacks are exploring an avenue that may offer greater promise. The vanguard mission of blacks in the Movement is, as we have seen, based in part on blacks being the group of the most evidently exploited. In addition to this basis, which is related to conventional notions of class warfare, the blacks have the assets of demonstrated moral virility, a capacity for social fury, and no alternative to radical action in order to gain wider recognition of their asserted identity. These three facts are interrelated but distinct.

Moral virility is unquestionably the force of Martin Luther King in American life. Others may cite Malcolm X, at whose funeral Ossie Davis declared, "He was our black prince. He was our black manhood!" Certainly King, however, was to most honorable men around the world the picture of the humanity to which we aspire. While his influence can obviously not be separated from his being black, it is important that in the consciousness of modern man his impact is not in exclusive terms of black humanity but of humanity. This is not a loss of blackness in the image but, quite the opposite, the strengthening of black identity through the process of universalization. That is, the blackness asserted is comprehended by the larger world and reinterpreted in an affirmative way back to the black community. It is of enormous significance that, after several years of carping remarks about King and his vision (beginning with the Meredith march of 1965), the most determined black leadership today has vigorously appropriated King in the Movement's hagiology.

The capacity for social fury is by definition undisciplined. Yet within the context of directed change it is indispensable. It is H. Rap Brown's, "We must move from resistance to aggression, from revolt to revolution. For every Huey Newton, there must be ten dead racist cops, and for every Black Death there must be a Dien Bien Phu. May the deaths of '68 signal the beginning of the end of this country." The fact that Brown seems to be discredited among much revolutionary black leadership today does not mean that the fury to which he gave vent is any less present in the black community.

Another factor supporting the vanguard mission of blacks is the fact that innumerable blacks are persuaded there is no alternative to radical action in order to gain recognition for their asserted identity. In *Dark Ghetto* Kenneth Clark explains the dynamics of urban violence:

> The Negro seemed to feel nothing could happen to him that had not already happened; he behaved as if he had nothing to lose. His was an oddly controlled rage that seemed to say, during those days of social despair, "We have had enough. The only weapon you have is bullets. The only thing you can do is to kill us." . . . His acts were a desperate assertion of his desire to be treated as a man. He was affirmative up to the point of inviting death; he insisted upon being visible and understood. If this was the only way to relate to society at large, he would die rather than be ignored.

Moral credibility, fury, and a readiness to die for recognition as a man are essential ingredients which white radicals see as distinctively present in the black liberation movement. Some white radicals, following James Forman's suggestion, succumb to the myth of black superior humanity. As asserted by Forman it is chauvinistic, when accepted by whites it is sycophantic and can lead only to a "diversionary and reactionary," and inevitably abortive, desire by whites to share in the mystique of being black. It has as much to do with radical change as does the IBM executive sitting down in his Westchester home to a dinner of "soul food" marketed by the A&P. In terms of social change, the affirmative mythologies of blackness are as destructive as the negative mythologies that have so long dominated the minds of black and white Americans. They encourage only new variations on black-white game playing. The Movement is better preoccupied with the hard economic, political, and ideological factors at the heart of social oppression.

The Peoples of Color

Another factor supporting the black's vanguard mission in change is black identification with the Third World. At first this too may seem to be largely mythological, and, as it is sometimes exhibited, it does have a fairy-tale quality. In Buffalo, New York, an eighteen-year-old black youth in an Anti-Draft Union meeting insisted, "I am here to speak for the oppressed peoples of the Third World" and argued that his sizable constituency entitled him to a larger vote in the meeting. In his mind the fact that he had never been outside the eastern United States did not make less credible his credentials as ambassador from Asia, Africa, and Latin America. The black man plays the role of universal surrogate. That is, he is the stand-in for the unrepresented. A curious twist on this surrogate role was evident in Sweden this past year during a visit I made with a number of black and white peace activists to the war resisters and American deserters in Stockholm. There is a small group of American blacks who have been in Sweden for several years, some from the early 1950s. There is an organization called SCAN-SNCC (Scandinavian SNCC) and the blacks were lionized by the students of the Swedish NLF (National Liberation Front to liberate Sweden). It became clear that radicals, frustrated by trying to promote revolution in eminently "successful" socialist Sweden, were holding tenaciously to these surrogate blacks who provided not only psychological contact with the Third World but, more importantly, vicarious participation in the experience of "American imperialist, capitalist, racist oppression."

In the Movement, however, the black association with the Third World does not rest on myths and games alone. There are at least four clear and factually rooted reasons for the association. First, the line between haves and have-nots is generally drawn between those who are identifiably "white" and the world's "peoples of color." The hegemony of Soviet-European-North American power over the rest of the world makes up the bulk of the model of exploitation, with additional support from such examples as South Africa, Rhodesia, and Australia. On the American scene, the blacks are the chief people of color. Second, there is the obvious biological history tying American blacks to Africa and thus, in psychological and political effect, to the Third World. Third, the American blacks have in the most fundamental and direct way been defined historically by white power. This experience of being the victim, or beneficiary, depending on one's viewpoint, of white power definition is an increasingly important factor in the consciousness of the peoples of Asia, Africa and Latin America.

Fourth, and quite evidently, the blacks present to Americans with inescapable immediacy the living witness to the consequences of the abuse of American power. In the debate on Vietnam, the black contention that America is as racist in its foreign policy as in its domestic became more plausible to many white Americans. In terms of U.S. power and prejudice, it is said, the Third World is synonymous with the niggers outside our gates. Thus it becomes a little less fantastic that the young man in Buffalo presumes "to speak for the oppressed peoples of the Third World."

Vital Minorities

Any effort to sketch the character and perimeters of the Movement must include the other racial minorities in the United States. The Indian Americans, neglected wards of a forgetful nation, have at present almost no role in the Movement, except as objects of concern and of illustration in standard speeches about genocide and racism. Efforts at organization have to date proved almost uniformly fruitless. Spanish-speaking Americans, Mexicans and Puerto Ricans, present an increasingly crucial challenge to the Movement. From the SCLC-organized Poor Peoples Campaign of spring 1968 and from Eldridge Cleaver in Algiers, 1969, the word has gone out that black liberation strategy must be shaped in alliance with Spanish-Americans. It is not yet determined that responsibility for effecting this coalition rests with the blacks. Aside from his ideological loyalty to Dr. King, César Chávez, to cite the most public example, has led his California insurgency depending more on white liberal-radical alliances than on black. In New York City with its more than one million Puerto Ricans there is an almost traditional despair about the possibilities of black-Puerto Rican alliances. On the electoral politics front, some strategists took heart in 1969 when Herman Badillo, a Puerto Rican, won strong majorities in all the black districts in the mayoralty primary. Similar signs of hope were perceived by some in Mexican-American support for the black opponent of Los Angeles' Mayor Yorty.

In New York City blacks and Puerto Ricans combined could hold effective political control of the city. But social change is not a matter of arithmetic, and even if the arithmetic could be translated into political power, an influential minority among both blacks and Puerto Ricans disdain such an effort in electoral politics as a distraction from the more radical changes required. To date there is no significant meeting between the self-consciously revolutionary elements of the two communities, and the several establishments of the City continue to be successful in playing one against the other. A further complication is that the white liberal can identify with the Mexican-American migrant workers struggle in a way that projects on to that struggle all the emotion and imagery of the civil rights movement pre-1965. One union organizer, just returned from a march and mass with César Chávez, remarked, "Man, it was great. Just like being back in Selma again."

In short, although there are obvious reasons suggesting that Spanish-speaking Americans should be closely associated with the radical insurgency of the blacks, it is not at all certain this will be the case. One, possibly compensating, side effect of this is that the Spanish thrust will recapture some of the significant white liberal enthusiasm for domestic change that fell away since 1965. It is just conceivable that even the labor unions will become less hostile to the Movement. White union money and resources in the California strikes, as well as in southern black labor efforts such as that of the hospital workers in Charleston, South Carolina, are important omens. Similarly, the black-Puerto Rican insurgencies in several New York City unions have rekindled some of the radical hopes that American unionism had before it was sold into its present bondage to the Great American Way.

Refugees from the Establishment

White youth, honorary youth, the Old Left, blacks, Spanish-Americans and the radicalized liberal, this is the constituency of the Movement. Political analyst Arnold Kaufman attempts to describe the last group in his perceptive book *The Radical Liberal, A New Man in American Politics*. Kaufman sees these non-young, non-black, non-poor participants in the Movement largely in continuity with the liberalism of the 1950s, of the John Kennedy era and, for that matter, of the New Deal. Notwithstanding that next to the military-industrial complex the liberal is the most popular scapegoat of radical rhetoric, these radicalized liberals constitute a major element in the Movement. Their financial resources and their influence in voluntary associations, public agencies, universities, churches, and the mass media are inestimable assets. Radical liberals are not agreed on strategy. Many favor non-violent, although definitely not "moderate," means of change, some for strategic and some for ideological reasons. Even among these there is a widespread belief that their personal and organizational commitment to non-violence will have to be augmented by violence carried out by others.

As in other countries and other revolutions, there is a small minority of the very wealthy thoroughly committed to the support of avowedly revolutionary action. The councils of black and white radicalism gather not only in ghetto store fronts and basement rooms on campus, but also in posh apartments on Chicago's North Shore and in New York's East Seventies. In the luxurious flat of a moneyed Chicago widow one radical recently explained that he has no qualms about associating with the rich. "I'm serious about revolution and I know you don't make a revolution without bread. Anyway, you can be sure of one thing, the pigs aren't going to try and bust this place."

Until he had to remove himself from the scene, one prominent black radical on the coast held frequent strategy sessions on the yacht of a California millionaire. The mogul in question explained his support, only half-jokingly, "This road is lined with beautiful estates like mine. Come the revolution, the rest of them are going to be Peoples' Palaces. I expect to live in mine."

The mention of this type of alliance is not intended to embarrass the Movement, although I suspect some people will consider it injurious. More injurious and embarrassing is the Movement's failure to respond to the fantasies of the Right about the Movement's sources of income. "Where do these radicals get their money?" is the persistent question raised about the airplane tickets and other expenses required for the innumerable gatherings, programs, and publications of the radical Left. The answer is nothing so dramatic as secret conduits from Moscow or Peking. In fact the Movement is for the most part run on a shoestring, with its organizations perpetually teetering on the edge of bankruptcy. Most Movement activities are supported by personal sacrifice in scrimping a few savings from meager jobs, skipping meals, and skill in evading bill collectors. Where, however, there is more substantial money it is good capitalist money raised in the best American tradition of voluntarism. Also the financing of American radicalism is "as American as cherry pie."

Some of the rich, like the Californian mentioned, are following one interpretation of Jesus' advice, "And I tell you, make friends for yourselves by means of unrighteous mammon, so that when it fails they may receive you into eternal habitations." (Luke 16) Or as a sympathetic eastern businessman put it, "Many of my friends thought the New Deal would destroy everything we had. The New Deal saved capitalism. The country's falling apart now, as far as I can see. Maybe radicalism is going to save

America." Such supporters may get more than they
bargained for from their revolutionary friends, but their
support is not as illogical or self-defeating as it may at
first seem. Others who make up the affluent base of support
are less calculating. As simplistic as it may seem, they
are apparently motivated by an altruistic conviction that
from him to whom much is given much is expected. They
understand the special responsibility of wealth to support
what they believe are the causes of social justice. Several
best-selling authors have assigned royalties to Movement
organizations. One businessman whose income is largely
from contracts with the Pentagon contributed over $75,000
directly in one year. Such support is often derided as
"conscience money" given in order to relieve guilt feelings,
but the radicals who distain the motives do not usually
scorn the cash.

Neither is it quite fair for those on the Left to criticize
organizations of the Right for being dependent on funds
from the plutocracy. One organization's reliance on enlightened generosity is another organization's sinister captivity to the military-industrial complex. Here I do not
have in mind the numerous "voluntary associations" directly and richly supplied by big labor, business associations and professional and industrial lobbies. These are
avowedly devoted to maintaining things more or less as
they are, although put to the wall they would probably
manifest a predominantly Rightist inclination. It is the
radically and explicitly Rightist groups, which are like the
radical Left in being set on a major restructuring of
American society, that have a similar base of financial
support. The most radical organizations of Left and Right
are prevented, by both self-understanding and necessity,
from relying entirely on membership financing through
dues and the such. Both look to the big money, and American socially concerned capitalists calculate their self-inter-
est, form their consciences and put their money, accord-
ingly, on the John Birch Society or the Progressive Labor
Party. The former no doubt does better than the latter,

but, over-all, it seems probable that the funds received by the radical Left compare favorably with those received by the radical Right.

The financial importance of all this is obvious. Not so widely recognized is the strategic importance. Suppression of the radical Left can no longer be achieved by raiding the headquarters of revolutionary organizations or by concocting criminal charges against its more visible activists, although these tactics will remain popular. Effective suppression will have to reach far into most of the major institutions and centers of influence in American life. The knowledge of this wider complicity makes some radical leaders less anxious than the liberal establishments about the imminence of an official and wholesale effort to "get" the Movement. This may also be an illusory sense of security, since anonymous friends in high places are careful to keep their options open. Complicity can be a compelling factor, but come the time of testing and most friends will calculate again and re-form their consciences in line with new exigencies.

The Radical Jew

The recent heated debate about black anti-Semitism makes necessary a specific discussion of the Jew in the Movement. Not only the blacks, but also whites for whom the blacks are the primary force of the Movement, feel called upon to take an attitude toward Jewish involvement in the struggle. Jewish student leaders, disproportionately strong in terms of the size of the Jewish population but not in terms of the Jewish tradition of social concern, have in some instances been torn between Jewish identity and a desire to embrace certain versions of the black world view. Such tensions were exacerbated, and to some extent created, by the United Federation of Teachers in

New York, which unconscionably exploited the Auschwitz reflex in its propaganda against black-led efforts to gain greater community control of the schools. The fears raised by these largely contrived charges of anti-Semitism were given a form of legitimation by articles in *Commentary* and pronouncements from synagogue councils. The gradual awareness that the UFT was less than a disinterested champion of the Jewish good name and the ferocity of the controversy that was sparked, however, soon occasioned serious rethinking in Jewish circles. Evidence of heavy Jewish voting for a reactionary candidate in the mayoralty race, widespread expressions of Jewish disillusionment with any involvement in black movements, and, most dramatically, the formation of an anti-black goon squad calling itself the Jewish Defense League had, by the end of 1969, caused the most influential persons and organizations in the Jewish community to call a moratorium on public debate about black anti-Semitism. Even the UFT and its president, Albert Shanker, having successfully secured their program through legislation, were calling for the rebuilding of a black-white coalition for urban change.

It is not clear how much or how deeply the Jewish community was influenced by the black anti-Semitism debate, or how many supporters of the Movement were alienated. Within the Movement, however, many of the scars are only lightly healed. The New York school confrontation opened up other questions which have complicated the Jewish role in the Movement. One question is reflected in the previously restrained but deeply felt resentment of a black leader who told me, "I'm tired of Jews saying how they're our best friends because nobody knows about suffering like they do. I'm tired of their exhibiting their wounds. We're the ones who're oppressed here. The Jew's doing all right here. Black suffering, not Jewish suffering, is the issue in America." The expression is no doubt insensitive, but it is important.

In the Maidanek concentration camp, according to

Alexander Donat's *Holocaust Kingdom,* Rabbi Schipper said, "But if *we* write the history of this period of blood and tears . . . who will believe us? Nobody will want to believe us, because our disaster is the disaster of the entire civilized world . . . We'll have the thankless job of proving to a reluctant world that we are Abel, the murdered brother." It seems impossible that job can ever be completed, yet it becomes increasingly thankless. For the white as well as the black radical, especially for the young, Maidanek and Treblinka often seem distant and "irrelevant." This poses what is surely one of the most painful problems facing the man whom Bruno Bettelheim calls "the interim Jew," who is neither a ghetto Jew nor an Israeli, but for whom the Holocaust remains definitive in his understanding of himself as a man. Rabbi Schipper weeps at the death of "the civilized world" and recognizes the Jew as Abel. But for many younger radicals, the demise of that "civilized world" is not tragedy but goal, for that world is the demonic force destroying the more immediate "Abels" of black America, Vietnam, and Arab Africa.

The Movement, especially the student sector, is regularly criticized for its lack of historical perspective. Only such a lack can explain the attitude that the Holocaust is irrelevant or at most a distant misfortune, rather than a persistently haunting parable revealing also *our* potential for social madness. This fault in the Movement is in curious contradiction to the virtually unanimous enthusiasm young radicals have for the judgments of the Nuremberg Tribunal and their teaching of personal responsibility. Nuremberg is, of course, inexplicable without reference to the Holocaust. Yet the widespread inability to identify with the Jewish experience of oppression cannot be explained simply in terms of inconsistency and historical myopia.

Jewish uneasiness about the Movement will be kept alive by two very real issues. One is the continuing encroachment of blacks on civil service and municipal jobs of all kinds. The other is the Middle East. The first is at the heart of the New York school dispute. It will not be the last contest that takes the form of a black versus a Jewish struggle for public jobs. The irony and root of the problem is that Jews are now being challenged for those positions they entered two and three decades ago for precisely the same reason that blacks are now pushing into public employment, because of discrimination in the so-called private sector. Milton Himmelfarb warns in a *Commentary* article, "In New York our remaining years in the civil service, and above all in the schools, are not many: if policy does not drive us out, terrorism will."

Also in the university, the establishment of a policy of quota systems for blacks is seen by most Jews as a direct onslaught against the meritocratic admission systems that have served Jews so well. Yet among radicals, reformists and revolutionaries alike, there seems to be a consensus in support of structural changes such as quotas, reparations, compensatory discrimination and the like. Reformists want these because our society seems to have decided that college education is both a right and a prerequisite for economic advance, and they see no other way in which most blacks will be admitted, given the "retarded start" program operated by urban schools. Revolutionaries want black college admissions increased because the campus is the training center and staging area, it is believed, for the final overthrow. For members of the Establishment, who can send their children to educational enclaves protected from mandated mediocrity, letting the college be incorporated into the public high school syndrome is a cheap enough price to pay to pacify black demands with the illusion of educational progress. Many Jews, who remember the quota as prelude to pogrom, feel they are being asked to bear the burden of the new order in civil service and education.

Compensatory policies to benefit blacks will almost certainly increase as a point of tension within the Movement.

The tension should promote more critical examination of the connection between real merit and the much-vaunted meritocracy, asking whether in fact the scales of merit are not weighted culturally against the black. The demythologizing in recent years of the culturally conditioned IQ tests can be a forerunner of a much more massive challenge to the criteria by which American society rates its citizens. These questions cannot be explored here, but their importance for the Movement is obvious, since the great majority of black and white activists is convinced that the foundational criteria of American meritocracy are used to exclude the black American. Those who challenge the criteria are naturally cool to programs aimed at "bringing black Americans up to standards," since such programs merely give the appearance of greater legitimacy to hopelessly skewed standards. There is still another debate with those who contend that any process of differentiation is dehumanizing and destructive of the kind of society for which the Movement should strive. Whether or not one agrees with C. P. Snow and others who argue that Jews are innately superior, the tradition of Jewish excellence in most fields of endeavor makes the polemic against differentiation-by-merit a difficult doctrine for Jews in the Movement.

Then there is the Middle East. Radical white and black affinity for the Arab belligerents needs no elaboration. At least since June 1967 Israel's being cast in the role of Abel seems implausible. For purposes of holding radical loyalties, nothing succeeds like failure. Nevertheless, the view that the State of Israel is an agent of U.S. imperialism, while widespread, is of doubtful practical influence in the Movement. It provides a certain ideological consistency for some radicals, since it is unthinkable that the U.S. could be on the right side of any Third World conflict. And this is not unimportant. But, apart from precluding unanimous public opinion in favor of Israel and apart from Arab countries providing a place of refuge for a few American radicals, the sympathy for the Arab

122 Richard John Neuhaus

states has no immediate strategic consequence for the Movement in the United States. Were Israel thrown on the defensive militarily or were U.S. ground forces to be employed in the Middle East, there would be a qualitatively new situation. Given these or other contingencies, I believe the sympathies of non-Jews in the Movement would prove unpredictable. As it is, the simultaneous debates about Vietnam and the Middle East have placed strains on the Movement but show no signs of destroying alliances. Except for the most dogma-oriented radicals, there is no insistence that Jews conform to revolutionary orthodoxy by abandoning their support of Israel. Similarly, few Jews in the Movement have felt compelled to declare themselves out of communion with those who disagree on the nature of justice in the Mideast. This solution of mutual tolerance is no doubt unsatisfactory, but it seems necessary at least for the present, and it should continue to be possible. Co-operation is based not on total agreement but on the conviction that groups have more in common than in conflict.

To speak about what Jews have in common with the Movement is grossly misleading. It suggests that there is a Movement apart from American Jews. There are of course movements within the Movement in which Jews have little part, but the Movement under discussion here is in continuity with an American radicalism that can no more be explained without reference to Jews than can the New York Police Department without reference to the Irish. If the Jewish community has not been the social conscience in American life, it is hard to know where that conscience might be located. To be sure, the temptations of class and social success take their toll, and Jews too join the resistance to needed change. People tire of being taken for granted, and some, as Milton Himmelfarb puts it, will begin to refuse to "pay for the delight of hearing black actors or activists fleer and menace whites, liberals, and Jews." But being taken for granted is the other side of being relied upon, even trusted. Resentment of being taken for granted is a poor reason to up the ante for co-operation.

Jews, individually and organizationally, have the job of working out whatever distinctly Jewish problems there are in being part of the Movement. Non-Jewish radicals have the job of not exacerbating those problems. Conflict between Jew and non-Jew is among the "reactionary and diversionary" tactics that weaken the challenge to the class structures and racist-militarist mentality that corrupt American life. Like most American whites, Jews too are reluctant to relinquish the notion that control of the Movement should be in proportion to contribution to the Movement. At the risk of generalizing, however, I would say that Jewish activists are more sensitive than most to the vanguard mission of the blacks. We can anticipate that a few self-indulgent radicals, black and white, will from time to time beat the broken drums of anti-Semitism, and that a few reactionary forces in the Jewish community will appear to march in time out of the Movement. The drum-beaters should be isolated and discredited, the marchers were never in the Movement. In spite of new and painful adjustments, the Movement can bring us closer to that new world which is, after all, a Jewish-biblical hope in which the rest of us share, as it were, by adoption.

The Jew is the elder brother who is learning not to act like an elder brother. The end result of the black anti-Semitism controversy can clarify and strengthen the Jewish role in the Movement. Clarify, because it demonstrates that, aside from the issue of Israel, the Jewish community does not conform to a single pattern of social behavior. Strengthen, because those Jews involved in the Movement have been more acutely sensitized to the pluralism of the Movement itself and are equipped to adapt to yet another phase in the ongoing effort to overcome the condescension that others, especially blacks, reject as subtle colonialism.

Agreement and Contradiction

It is difficult to find a common vision, a specific idea of
the new order, that holds the Movement together. As we
have seen, when such ideas are articulated they can result
in diametrical oppositions. There are programs of radical
action to make the American promise, given in the Declaration of Independence and other founding documents,
finally work. Others see the same radical action leading
toward a hoped-for revolution, and that revolution is in
turn projected in various and contradictory versions. Yet
others say it is not necessary or possible to present a
blueprint for the new order. Some who take this view
profess confidence in the power of the future itself to
produce that genuinely new thing required for man's humanization. Others publicly agree that a blueprint should
not be offered, but privately admit to a rather specific
notion of the future, but one they believe most of the
Movement is not yet ready to accept. In this strange collection of contradictions, we may wonder what is the body
of doctrine, or even cluster of attitudes, that holds together something solid enough to be called the Movement.

One doctrine is that Vietnam is not a distortion but a
symptom of the use of American power. The U.S. is fundamentally and relentlessly hostile to the world's poor becoming the artisans of their own destinies. It is not the
exception but the rule that U.S. power is aligned with repressive regimes in the Third World, all under the guise of
combating communism. A growing "revisionist" literature
suggest that the Cold War itself is largely a U.S. invention
designed to provide cover for the military and economic
policies required to maintain imperial interests in weaker
nations and to distract attention from domestic injustices.
The real struggle is not between Communist and "free"

world, the latter being in fact far from free, but between rich and poor, and there is no doubt about which side the United States is on.

Another doctrine is that what happened at the Democratic National Convention in Chicago 1968 is not a distortion but a symptom of the way American politics operates. The brutal police action against protest was a moment of truth, repeated many times over in other confrontations with the Movement and revealing to white and affluent Americans the realities of abusive power normally reserved for the black and poor. The Convention's disdain for the popular will expressed in the Kennedy and McCarthy primary victories was only a particular clumsy manifestation of the political system's bankruptcy. The parties are designed and manipulated to prevent rather than to facilitate popular participation in decision-making. Efforts to reform the parties are probably bad because they extend credibility to the political system more than they effect meaningful change. Further participation by radicals in electoral politics can only distract energies from the more basic structural changes that are urgently needed.

Another set of doctrinal theses is related to the future of the black man. These include the notion that nonviolent appeals to conscience are futile because in all probability the society has no conscience. It is further asserted that the gap between black and white is, by every index of benefit and opportunity, widening rather than narrowing. If evidence is suggested to the contrary, the response is that every "advance" by the black man is in fact a tightening of the noose, assuring that blacks will hang with whites in a society that is surely headed toward destruction.

A fourth cluster of attitudes has to do with appropriate strategies to effect change, allowing that the only really worthwhile change might be to bring the society down. "From dialogue to protest to resistance to revolution" is the usual way of expressing the radical development. For many in the Movement these four postures are not mutually exclusive. Active support for resistance, especially as it relates to undermining the draft system, is probably the most widely acknowledged line between liberal and radical. The civil rights movement's conscientious violation of racial segregation laws must be extended to the legal and political system as a whole. The law and order that is the servant of prevailing injustices must be desacralized and delegitimized. Whether by violence or disruption, the society's institutions must be made vulnerable to change, they must be prevented from going on with business as usual. The major institutions, like the political system itself, have clearly demonstrated that they have neither the will nor the means for critical participation and correction from within.

Sets of doctrines or attitudes could be multiplied and broken down beyond these four. What according to Jerome Skolnick in *Politics of Protest* was true of the peace movement at one point applies to the entire Movement phenomenon: "The more one learns about the organizational structure and development of the . . . movement, the more reluctant one must be to speak of its concerted direction." With respect to the points mentioned above, there are those, for instance, who are engaged, perhaps skeptically and reluctantly, in trying to change the Democratic Party or in keeping alive the hope for issue-oriented parties that can bring honesty to the electoral process. Just as certainly there are those in the Movement who reject all the allusions to strategic violence, insisting that militant non-violence, far from being outmoded, has not yet been given fair trial. Other variations are evident enough, giving support to the expectation that no tests of orthodoxy will be imposed in the near future.

Yet, as the lady says, "We know who the 'we' is and we know who the 'they' is." "We" are those who are in fundamental sympathy with the theses sketched above, prepared to tolerate variations in how these consensus insights should be implemented, and are active in groups that understand themselves to be distinct from the creed of the liberal establishments. "We" are those who believe the pressure must be intensified; we cannot succumb to the liberal fear of repression which, in order to allay reaction, surrenders in advance the freedom of action which repression would deny. "We" are those *who think of ourselves* as the Movement, a floating association of "persons, organizations, worldviews and activities located on what is conventionally called the Left and acting in radical judgment upon the prevailing patterns, political, economic, social and moral, of American life."

"We" are for revolution. A revolution of consciousness, no doubt. A cultural revolution, certainly. A non-violent revolution, perhaps. An armed overthrow of the existing order, it may be necessary. Revolution for the hell of it or revolution for a new world, but revolution, Yes.

A Revolutionary Consciousness

The phenomenon is undeniable, what it means is subject to interpretation. It is the growth of a revolutionary consciousness in American life, and the Movement is its prophet. The revolutionary consciousness is in part a mood, to a lesser extent a program. It is the feeling that the times have brought things to a head, things cannot go on as they are.

The political significance of this consciousness is frequently dismissed. Psychologists note that the feeling of historical uniqueness, the intuition of impending events of unprecedented impact, is endemic to youth. Only the young, it is said, have not been ravaged by cynicism. They alone hold dreams inviolate. The hope for radical change is an indulgence that only the innocent can afford. But the Movement is more than the young. And, even with regard to the youth sector, the psychological explanation fails to do justice to the phenomenon. A St. Louis professor was explaining, and explaining away, the campus insurrection in terms of "youthful rebellion." "That's exactly what we're talking about," interrupted a student, "that's your way of making it seem like the problem's with us instead of the university. That's what you call rational explanation, but it's just clever evasion. In fact it's not even very clever any more, it's just standard hypocrisy dressed up like objectivity."

Whether the hypocrisy is standard or redesigned in response to a new situation, it has lost its power to discredit the radical conviction. Few young people and fewer over thirty deny the impact of hidden and overt psychological dynamics shaping the Movement. But they protest those analyses that distract from and tend to dissipate the emphatically political character of radicalism. Any explanation of the Movement is suspect as "reductionist" that does not first take seriously the Movement's professed intent to bring about radical change. No matter how skilled the explanation, it cannot evade the self-evident fact that hundreds of thousands of Americans believe this society needs revolution. That is in itself of momentous political significance, regardless of its alleged dynamics. Nor can even the most evasive explanation credibly claim that radical protest can be explained by forces emanating from the Movement itself. Revolutionary consciousness is not a creation *ex nihilo* nor is it immaculately conceived.

The failure to permit the fulfillment of black identity and potential, the militarization of the society, the unresponsiveness of the political system, the inability even to conceive of an American role in stemming world famine, the decay of urban areas, the emptiness of technological success in space and affluence in the suburbs, Vietnam, Vietnam, and Vietnam—these are not the inventions of the Movement. They are not ghostly apparitions conjured for the purpose of radicalizing the society. They are part of a long list of failures that compel people to the conclusion that this is a failing social order. Some black Americans may be spared the feeling of deep disillusionment, of which James Baldwin wrote in *The Fire Next Time*:

> The American Negro has the great advantage of having never believed that collection of myths to which white Americans cling [when this was written, 1963]; that their ancestors were all freedom-loving heroes, that they were born in the greatest country the world has ever seen, or that Americans are invincible in battle and wise in peace, that Americans have always dealt honorably with Mexicans and Indians and all other neighbors or inferiors, that American men are the world's most direct and virile, that American women are pure.

There are enclaves in which James Baldwin's description of white America's self-understanding seems plausible, in American Legion halls and among the "new" Republicans of the South. Perhaps the majority of Middle America, what conservatives like to call "the heartland," still accepts the description. But an "enclave" attitude is not defined by a nose count that determines it is held by a minority of Americans. The attitudes of an intellectually and culturally sterile majority can be reshaped by an aggressive and creative minority. It is not so much a matter of *how many* are disillusioned with the existing order as of *who* is disillusioned.

An inordinate influence in how a society understands itself is exercised by the intellectuals who mint the metaphors and those in the media who promulgate them. The same weight in the scales of social effectiveness cannot realistically be assigned to the young and activist, on the one side, and to the old and indifferent on the other. It is true that in the existing order the latter often outweigh the former. But the fragility of the existing order is increased in exact ratio to the frequency with which that truth is demonstrated. The more blind and brutal the response to change, the more naked the display of power, the less real power possessed by the existing order. This observation is supposedly a commonplace, but it is clearly not common in the places where decisions are made. The bloodied clubs of frenzied police continue to be an effective organizing instrument for the Movement.

Less than a decade ago, but it seems in another epoch, John F. Kennedy announced that citizens should ask themselves, What can I do for my country? Incredibly enough, it seemed credible then, and millions of Americans, young and old, spoke without embarrassment about service to American purposes in the world. Eight years later, Senator Robert Kennedy evoked hopeful response with his call to "seek a newer world." The assumption of national righteousness had become implausible, but the hope was extended that perhaps United States power could be switched to the right side of the world revolution.

The loss of confidence grows among a large and influential sector of the American public who choose not to close their eyes to the oppressive uses of American power. In their eyes America is not the breaker but the welder of the chains of enslavement. They doubt that all the reform movements combined can do little more than sustain false hope for the healing of an irredeemably corrupt system. By congressional criticism of the military budget one or two of the Pentagon's more outrageous programs are less lavishly funded than the generals wish. Foreign aid builds a handful of schools in Latin America, which results in conditioning bourgeois counterrevolutionaries in lands that cry for revolution. The reformists applaud more black "firsts" in public life, business, and the entertainment world (soon there may be four blacks with their own network program), for all of which the black masses should feel a pride that takes the mind off degrading schools, housing, medical care, and welfare systems that conspire to deprive them of their humanity. And if you are troubled by conditions that imperil planet

Earth, find patriotic comfort in America's mature acceptance of its world responsibility, symbolized by napalm, torture, and the presence of U.S. counterinsurgency teams in more than thirty countries where we insure political stability against the subversive impatience of the wretched of the earth. Albert Camus yearned for a country that an honorable man could love and love justice too. The most lively and socially committed sector of our population is persuaded that the United States is not such a country.

This Time Things Are Different

This is not the first time there has been a widespread disillusionment among Americans about America. Already in 1914, Walter Lippmann wrote about the sense of drift that pervaded American life. We dignified this sense of drift, this feeling that we are victims and not masters of historical circumstance, he said, by terming it liberalism. There had been the Revolutionary period, succeeded by the National period, in both of which there was a plausible and encompassing rationale for the American experiment. The Civil War came in time to distract attention from troubling doubts, but the doubts emerged again through industrialization, urbanization, and other fundamental changes for which history supplied no ideological framework.

By 1914 the doubts seemed inescapable, but again we escaped by closing ranks for war. Critical reflection stood little chance of getting a hearing during the "high" of the nineteen twenties exhilarated by a sense of peace and unaccustomed prosperity. The collapse of the thirties opened the floodgates of radical criticism and hungry people were treated to an infinite variety of Utopian ideas and revolutionary programs in lieu of bread. As the popular and radical critique approached the nerve center of the system, however, a partially revived economy was strengthened by war, which again came to the rescue. Since 1947 and the Truman Doctrine ("It must be the policy of the United States to support free peoples who are resisting attempted subjugation by armed minorities or by outside pressures.") the prevailing order has been sustained by a state of permanent warfare. Now Vietnam has not ended the Cold War but it has decisively ended the Cold War as a politically plausible context for the definition of national purpose.

We are back again with the "drift" of 1914. There is no war, and it is inconceivable that there can be a war which will solidify more than it divides the American people. Unlike the nineteen twenties and thirties, economic prosperity is neither a distracting novelty nor an overriding concern that can answer the questions now raised. The issues, so long sublimated, can no longer be ignored. Liberalism drifts in smug self-satisfaction, preening itself with its pragmatic and value-free cleverness in social problem-solving. In academia and in the councils of public power, political philosophy in the tradition of Western thought is moribund, if not already interred. The time for radicalism has struck. The stage is set and the casting offices have announced auditions for the event of the season, "Revolution."

Politics of Accommodation

Not everyone who auditions for Revolution can be expected to show up for the manning of the barricades. This is not due only to a failure of nerve. There are within the Movement differing ideas about the appropriate response to radicalism's moment. For each an argument can be made and, no matter which a person chooses, it is good to understand the options he rejects. In what follows we will focus on armed revolution and the questions that attend that option. But first we must understand why some participants are and will be coming out at different points, although they share in the Movement's pervasive revolutionary consciousness.

Some, and this is a probable majority of the Movement, will decide to work, as they say, "within the system." It is both unfair and inaccurate to view this choice as being in every instance a betrayal or cop-out. Sympathy is in order. And not only sympathy, which implies condescension, but an honest evaluation of the forces that compel so many to this choice. The younger radical, for instance, is forced to make a new decision when faced with the new situation of financial responsibility for a family. This situation usually marks the exit door from the youth culture. Critics of the Movement find comfort in their suspicion that the young radical will follow their form and shed his radicalism when he assumes his "responsibilities." There will unquestionably be many instances to confirm the suspicion. Our generation, like other generations, has a greater capacity for security than for adventure. And we have not fully estimated the devious achievement of the American Way, with its lures, rewards, and sanctions, if we are still shocked by people selling out.

Others will maintain their radical critique in spite of formidable pressures to conform. They will conclude that the United States is not in fact in a pre-revolutionary stage. They will agree with the judgment of some historians that successful reform can have revolutionary results, while abortive revolutions bring only frustration and repression. They will add that such reforms must be radical reforms, disrupting the values and patterns of convenience. But the emphasis will be on continuity rather than discontinuity, aimed not so much at bringing to fruition the revolutionary potential of American political history as at simply fulfilling the promises that America has explicitly made. In all this they will be

working, and when put to the wall will admit they are
working, within the system. To prevent the system from
becoming more oppressive, they say, it is necessary to
oppose it radically. But the intention is clearly to reform
and, if possible, to redeem what is. In the absence of
more Vietnams—and even the Pentagon is not likely to
re-enact that drama in its universally repulsive form—it is
inevitable that many of the radicalized liberals in the
Movement will take a kinder view of possibilities for what
they will call radical reform of the system.

Those who are now posturing can be expected to revert
or progress to another style. The literary stars and denizens of the cocktail circuits will in large part withdraw
at the touch of serious repression. Or, if not out of fear,
they will act out of boredom, going on to something else
when fashionable people agree that "the revolution thing
has been done." In short, whether because the cost is too
high or the scene unfashionably dull, one should not expect
to meet all his Movement friends at the barricades.

Too Radical for Revolution

Yet others will not show up at the barricades because
they are too radical for revolution. The change they want
is not contained in any political ideology of Left or Right
nor susceptible to any political program. They are not
apolitical so much as anti-political. The goal is personal
and communal fulfillment, and politics in all its incarna-
tions is the enemy. The fast-developing cult of encounter
groups on the coast, the style of much "guerrilla thea-
ter," the spread of experimental communes from Big Sur
to Pennsylvania, and Ray and Alice's church up in
Stockbridge, Massachusetts, bear witness against the dehumanizing politicization of the whole of life.

This too is part of the Movement. The participant in

1970's commune was more than likely on 1968's picket line. He protested the war and the draft with a fervent "Hell no, we won't go!" and "Not with my life you don't!" But even then these were not so much political slogans in the conventional sense as a protest against politics as such, against an enterprise that presumes to subordinate personal values and relationships to programs, good and bad, of public policy. The suspicion that politics is sordid, exploitative, and humanly unsatisfying is, of course, shared by many Americans who cannot be considered radical. But for the radical who is graduated from the caldron of Movement politics, it goes much deeper.

Anti-politics is comparable to the *via negativa* of those who search for God. That is, the mystic moves beyond the conventional language and practices of religion. He pursues a theology not of God's presence but of his absence. Or it can be compared to what Susan Sontag describes as the "esthetics of silence." Art, she says, tends toward anti-art as the earnest artist becomes disillusioned with the tools, styles, and experiments of his work. They are no longer instruments but obstacles to what he yearns for, until finally he sees art as something to be overthrown. So the radical personalist and communalist would not change the political system or replace it with another but overthrow the despotic hold of politics on man's hopes. The new man will be brought into being not by politics but by liberation from politics.

There is no political program to liberate people from politics. Yet there is something one can do. It is emphatically not "dropping out" but an entering into possibilities of personal and communal experience. The pharmaceutical mysticism of the drug scene is a part of it that looms inordinately large in the minds of critics. The entire personalist and communalist venture is distressingly irrelevant to those who see the Movement solely as a political instrument. But to its devotees it is gloriously, liberatingly irrelevant. In its irrelevance is its guarantee against being captured by some foreigner's program for change. Those involved say they are making a "cultural revolution" or a "revolution in human consciousness." It is beyond politics but not indifferent to society. Some participants believe they are building a refuge to which people from the Movement can resort when they too have seen the futility of political programs and passions. Others have more ambitious and Utopian goals of a society, and perhaps all mankind, turned on to the infinite joys of being human.

The American system has been quick to capitalize on this development. A strong argument can be made that much of the "cultural revolution" is little more than a new faddishness filling the coffers of American business by producing new fashions, musical and literary tastes, and psychedelic styles for the advertising media. Confirmation of this thesis can be found in the teenie-bopper center of any medium-sized city or at the box offices of a dozen New York shows which, while purportedly revolutionizing the culture, must certainly satisfy their distinctly non-revolutionary producers.

The personalist-communitarian direction of part of the Movement may, some argue, be worse than frivolous and delusive. It directly strengthens the most destructive dynamics of American capitalism. In *One-Dimensional Man,* Herbert Marcuse condemns the instrument of "de-sublimation" by which criticism of the prevailing order is neutralized. The most radical protest, the most bizarre behavior, the most grating screed of the alienated is not repressed or punished. Diverse opinion or behavior when sublimated maintains its integrity and therefore, presumably, its danger to society. So, according to Marcuse, the cleverly exploitative social order encourages de-sublimation, welcomes even the most radical criticism as another factor that enriches the variety of experiences and therefore demonstrates the superiority of the System. Thus toleration is the enemy most to be feared by revolutionaries.

Those in the anti-political sector of the Movement, however, are trying something of significance far beyond what is suggested by the beads, posters, hair, and pot that have been so thoroughly co-opted. And mixed with America's cheap exploitation of the hippie scene is a perhaps unconscious hope that the alumni of politics will succeed. The successful middle-upper-middle-class American is neither so secure nor so satisfied as some Leftist polemics picture him. "The Organization Man," "The Gray Flannel Suit," "The Lonely Crowd," "The Status Seekers," enrich his everyday vocabulary of self-disdain. Hoping against hope and in spite of his knowledge of the failures that have gone before, he too yearns for a new community uncorrupted by relentless competition and the making of deals to survive. There is precious little happening in America that witnesses to the possibility of a radically different and liberating life style. There is nothing that provides the referent for judgment and provocation provided, for example, by monasticism in the Middle Ages. So, while some are busy exploiting "the cultural revolution" for selfish gain, others try to protect and nurture it as a tender plant that may yet become the Tree of Life.

The personalist-communitarian sector of the Movement is only now being recognized in its distinctiveness. Thus it does not play a large part in the previous description of the Movement's origins and constituency. In times of dramatic conflict between the forces of good and evil, such as during the protest against the Vietnam war, distinctions are blurred and the personalist-communitarians are inseparable from the radical politicians. Now it seems their numbers are growing. Their social marginality is by design and not necessarily the measure of importance. It is just barely conceivable that these gentle experiments in community may form the creative subculture from which will come the American Revolution of our century. Clearly, there is a growing number of people who are prepared to gamble on that possibility.

Non-violent Revolution

The future of the Movement, then, will rest with the politics of accommodation and with the anti-politics of the personalist-communitarians. But that is only part of the Movement now and in the years ahead, and it is impossible to say how large a part. The great majority of those who now consider themselves part of the Movement dissociate themselves from both options we have discussed. They want to be part of something else, an intensified thrust for a radical political alternative. In this connection we will consider armed revolution. First, however, there is yet another clearly radical and clearly political alternative. It is usually termed non-violent revolution. It differs from armed revolution not only in the means used but also in the ends sought. Indeed basic to non-violent revolution is the belief that ends and means are inseparable. "The means is the end in process of becoming."

Non-violence gets a bad press in radical circles today. Organizations such as the Southern Christian Leadership Conference and Movement publications such as *WIN*, issued from New York City, are frequently forced into being apologetic about their rejection of violence. The word "non-violence" itself seems negative, weak, spineless. Synonyms are used. The idea of non-violence runs counter to conventional notions of virility. Young men, black and white, profess to believe the choice between violence and non-violence has something to do with their balls. Much of the language in favor of violence is reminiscent of Georges Sorel's *Reflections on Violence* (1908), a book later used by Benito Mussolini and other fascists, although Sorel himself was an unconventional French Marxist. "Revolutionary violence" is contrasted with the "coercive force" of the state, the one is redemptive and the other the enemy of freedom. While Sorel is for the most part unknown in today's Movement, the line of thought is well represented in the writings of Frantz Fanon, Régis DeBray, and others and is incarnate in the imagery surrounding Malcolm X and Ernesto Che Guevara. All this forms the difficult context in which non-violent revolution must make its case.

There can be, however, no simple equation of militancy and violence. The most "militant" actions of recent years have often been undertaken by those who are ideologically non-violent. The politics of confrontation with the military and other power elites have been refined by pacifists in a long history of militant activism. Before the Vietnam war was an issue, pacifists sailed into nuclear testing zones, tied up munitions factories, organized tax resistance groups and obstructed congressional hearings with sit-ins and counterspectacles. Pacifists boarded naval vessels, chained themselves to AWOL soldiers and, in the last few years, led raids on draft boards, burning registration cards with napalm and covering files with blood. Roger Laport and Norman Morrison immolated themselves, one before the United Nations and the other at the Pentagon. Both were pacifists.

The point is that readiness to take radical action is not contingent upon an affirmation of violence. Indeed, were it useful to do so, exactly the opposite argument could be made on the basis of Movement experience to date. Black violence in the riotous insurrections in the cities is of a different kind. Most black leadership, whether violent or non-violent in orientation, recognizes the non-ideological and non-strategic character of black urban violence in the past. We will have occasion later to consider the developing signs of strategic violence, or political violence, in urban areas. Our purpose here is simply to correct the false equation of militancy with violence, and thus to help the non-violent revolutionaries get a better hearing.

Sober revolutionaries are interested not in posturing but in change. The goal of the Movement is neither vengeance nor virility but change. In "On Revolution and Equilibrium" Barbara Deming, a non-violent revolutionary, concludes that "those who say that they believe in nonviolence [must] learn to challenge more boldly those institutions of violence that constrict and cripple our humanity . . . Those who have questioned nonviolence [must] come to see that one's rights to life and happiness can only be claimed as inalienable if one grants, in action, that they belong to all men." The choice, it is urged, is not between a humble appeal to conscience or the seizing of power through violent force; non-violence has not failed, it has hardly been tried. Perhaps so. But perhaps also it is too late, or too early as the case may be, for non-violent strategy.

I was personally convinced, through working with Dr. King and his aides, that the Poor Peoples Campaign of spring 1968 would have been the most important test of revolutionary non-violence in the American experience. What the Poor Peoples Campaign became as a result of the shocked confusion surrounding Dr. King's death does not, I am confident, refute the above statement. The action was to be carefully phased into strategies of mounting militancy that would have, quite simply, prevented the nation's business from being conducted in Washington, if that was what was required to get response to the demands of the poor. Understandings and even alliances had been reached with the various black groups in Washington that did not share SCLC's non-violent ideology. The revolutionary content of the Poor Peoples Campaign was the demand that in effect the Bill of Rights be extended to include not only political and legal but also economic rights. Dr. King's call for "Rights in life as well as law" was not empty rhetoric but a carefully reasoned demand that, if successful, would have had revolutionary consequences for the redistribution of American power.

The Poor Peoples Campaign did not come off. But it is not futile to recall what might have been, for the memory of what might have been is sometimes the intuition of what might be. Surely it was a dream. The most imaginative political programs are born from dreams and return to dreams again. It is probably impossible to contribute anything new to what has been said about Martin Luther King and his death. I am persuaded that, if man prevails, another generation will still be searching for the words to express the loss.

No Other Choice

But now we must turn our attention to violent revolution. This is the last, and perhaps the most rapidly accelerating, movement within the Movement. Truth spoke to power and power was deaf. Love appealed to power and power was heartless. Humility petitioned power and power was cruel. Reason argued with power and power was stupid. Now violent power must address violent power.

Wise men who subscribe to violent revolution come to the position reluctantly, confessing they had no other choice. Witless men come to the position rashly, boasting they had no other thought. Whether wise or witless, they should be taken seriously. Much of the world is caught up in the anguish and hope of violent revolution. The proposal of violent revolution, in view of the numbers and influence of those who propose it, is a major social and political fact also in American life.

2. The Revolution

Just Feeling Radical

"The only pure acts left are violence and revolution," declares the student hero of Lindsay Anderson's film "If . . ." It is said to the throbbingly beautiful background music of the Sanctus from the Congolese "Missa Luba." This is the vengeance-virility-purity triumvirate that dominates much current discussion about revolution. Our purpose here is to challenge that dominance, to clear our minds, and examine revolution as a political program for change.

We also set aside frivolous or, at best, misleading language about revolution. In *Prophetic Voices: Ideas and Words on Revolution*, Freya Stark writes: "I like to contemplate revolution as something [we] undertake for fun . . . It should be a pleasant operation, and it is only because we have fallen into the habit of contemplating its grim side only that our attitude to revolution has come to be unfriendly." It may be nice to contemplate revolution her way, but it is not the revolution under discussion here. Neither is our subject *Revolution for the Hell of It* in which Abbie Hoffman, the jester of those excluded from the court, celebrates his insight that ". . . action is the only reality; not only reality, but morality as well . . . Confusion is mightier than the sword . . . By allowing all: loving, cheating, anger, violence, stealing, trading, you become situation oriented, and as such become more effective." Nazi SS troops, the Green Berets, and Marshal Ky are among the effective situation-oriented folk who readily agree.

Nor can we treat seriously the kind of revolution proposed by a black man who declares himself a candidate for mayor of Detroit. Running against another black man, he says, "The difference is that mine will be the only really revolutionary campaign." Campaigns to win elective office are by definition not revolutionary. At most they might promise rapid change, but rapid change within the system should not be confused with revolution. Finally, while the revolution is violent, not all violence is revolutionary. Violence might be used, and in American life frequently is used, to express a grievance. It may be helpful, as many people believe is the case with the riotous insurrections in the cities, to focus wider attention upon an injustice. But the logic of such violence, far from being revolutionary implies a confidence that the prevailing order will take steps to redress the grievance, if it is sufficiently inconvenienced by violent protest. Ironically, some who advocate violence on this level betray a greater confidence in American ways than do the liberals who are persuaded that violent inconveniencing of the society will provoke only brutal repression. Or, even more strange, the radical confidence may be in the much despised liberals themselves. One white radical, confronted with the conventional liberal argument about repression, replied, "Our job is to pressure the society, using violence if necessary. Yours [the liberals'] is to prevent the reaction. Handling the repression is your thing."

Revolution may focus on goods, institutions, or values, or all three. The black and poor revolution is in large part a revolution for goods. The poor want a fair share of what the society provides. Such issues as community control of public facilities and efforts to free minority issues from majority political control focus on institutions. The revolution of values is evident in the assertion of black culture and in the affluent white radical's search for a post-prosperity and post-technological life style. The student who says, "You don't know how bad things are unless you live in Scarsdale!" is clearly not desirous of more of the society's goods, nor, aside from personally threatening institutions such as the draft, is he directly concerned about the society's institutions. He is very much interested in changing the values, ranging from sexual behavior to the criteria of personal fulfillment. The commingling and confusion of these revolutionary thrusts have tended to deprive the word "revolution" of useful meaning. The statement "I am for revolution" thus often means little more than that the speaker is feeling radical at the moment.

Revolution for Real

Revolution is the use of armed force to effect fundamental change in the social and political order. This, at least, is what a growing number of Americans mean when they express their support for revolution, and this is what is meant by revolution in the pages following. The most current but by no means the only frame of reference for understanding revolution is that suggested by Marxist theory and experience. Such revolution intends to be all-encompassing, fundamentally changing institutions and values as well as redistributing goods. More accurately, at least according to Marxist theory, the economic change will produce the institutional and moral changes required for the new order. In any case, revolution aims at a total transformation of the society's power basis.

Effecting fundamental change means changing the "fundaments" of the society. Politically, this means in the United States replacing the Constitution. Change carried out within the context of constitutional government, or that leaves the U. S. Constitution as an authoritative point of political reference, is something less than revolution. Similarly, change that does not fundamentally alter the structures of economic control and distribution of wealth is something less than revolution. It is theoretically possible, although not in Marxist thought, for a revolutionary government to maintain such elements as an independent judiciary, authoritative legislative assembly, laws protecting private property and so forth. The mention of these elements suggests the magnitude of the issues involved in serious revolution. Those who are talking about change within the constitutional framework or transformations of lesser magnitude would do better to avoid confusing their programs, many of them no doubt radical, with revolution. Conditions in American life are indeed coming to a head and revolutionary plans are too serious to permit further confusion about what is proposed.

What follows is addressed especially to those who are earnestly engaged, and to those who are considering engagement, in revolutionary plans or actions involving the use of armed force to effect fundamental change in the social and political order. It is not written so much to encourage or discourage such engagement, but to clarify some of the issues to be thought through. What is said here may apply to revolution in any part of the world but is particularly related to the prospect of revolution in the United States of America. The following pages assume agreement with the Founding Fathers on the moral and political right to revolution, namely that "When government violates the rights of the people, insurrection is for the people, and for every portion of the people, the most sacred of rights and the most indispensable of duties." As Abraham Lincoln put it in his first inaugural address: "This country, with its institutions, belongs to the people who inhabit it. Whenever they shall grow weary of the existing government, they can exercise their constitutional right to amend it, or their revolutionary right to dismember or overthrow it."

Revolution and Responsibility

No word seems so hostile to the revolutionary spirit as does the word "responsibility." Most youth have never encountered the word except in the context of an adult urging them to conform. For radicals "responsibility" is a value to which the Establishment appeals to cool the action. Being responsible and being revolutionary are mutually contradictory, or so it seems. But we should not let the opposition have all the good words.

Responsibility means the ability to respond. The responsible person is a whole person living in lively resonance to the values, ideas, hopes and, above all, persons that shape his life situation. The opposite of being a responsible person is being an erratic, capricious, desultory, untrustworthy and vacillating person. Responsible is not the opposite of radical. The radical lives and works in spirited response to injustice and to the anguish of the world's oppressed. It is the Establishment that is irresponsible, incapable of responding, so trapped is it in inherited behavior patterns and enslaved by serving expediency. The radical is responsible to the realities of ideas and values and, most of all, to the reality of the oppressed. The radical has made the gut commitment to hold himself accountable to the poor.

The rebel, writes Carl Oglesby in *Containment and Change*, "is an irresponsible man whose irresponsibility has been decreed by others . . . He has no real views about the future . . . His motivating vision of change is, at root, a vision of something absent." The rebel cannot be engaged in "responsible exchange" about the issues. "The rebel is an incorrigible absolutist who has replaced . . . all solutions with the single irreducible demand that . . . those who now have all power shall no longer have any, and that those who now have none—the people, the victimized—shall have all . . . 'What do you want?' asks the worried, perhaps intimidated, master. 'What can I give you?' But the rebel answers, 'I cannot be purchased.' The answer is meant mainly to break off the conference."

Oglesby's remarks must be carefully qualified. There are times when the call to "responsibility" is in effect a call to abandon a radical course and submit to the conventional exchanges and controls by which the society makes decisions. In such instances, it may be strategically necessary to play the role of being "irresponsible" in order to sharpen the conflict and to avoid being trapped in the endless argumentation that marks "rational discourse." But there is an important difference between strategically choosing to play the irresponsible role and being in fact an irresponsible person.

Another qualification that must be made is that Oglesby, Fanon, and popular writers on revolution are often describing the *psychology* of the rebel. When it is said, for instance, that the rebel has no real idea of the new order for which he is struggling, this is a descriptive and not a prescriptive statement. In fact revolutionary forces, particularly the poor and illiterate, are motivated more by passion, indignation, and sheer rage than by any revolutionary analysis of the prevailing order and the hoped-for future. It is one thing to identify with the non-rational passions of the rebel in Algeria or Bolivia. It is another and ludicrous thing for the reader of this book to indulge in the primitivist fancy that he can or should operate mentally and emotionally as a Bolivian peasant. Such an effort is patronizing toward the peasant and, equally as bad, an exercise in false consciousness that can only distort the process by which the college-educated product of American society thinks through the prospect of revolution.

It has been further argued, however, that there is a self-authenticating revolutionary morality and revolutionary reasoning. This means the revolutionary cannot be "responsible" except in the context of the revolution itself, there are no points of reference outside the revolution by which the revolution can be evaluated. Thus Andrew Kopkind writes in *The New York Review,* "Morality, like politics, starts at the barrel of a gun." This suggests a kind of circular reasoning. To call it revolutionary reasoning is an insult to the revolution. The man says, Join the revolution because the revolution is right. You answer, How do I know the revolution is right? He says, Join the revolution (thereby agreeing the revolution is right) and you will agree with me the revolution is right.

The same kind of argument is used by some religious groups to persuade doubters to suspend their critical faculties. Every radical has encountered it in dealing with various establishments. If you accept the System's definitions of the problem and of what it means to be responsible, then you will find yourself agreeing that things should remain as they are. Whether it is used by a college administration or by a recruiter for the revolution, it is the same circular and evasive rationality, betraying intellectual bankruptcy.

Another ploy in the same game is to say that the values by which right and wrong can be determined are not now existing, either in the present system or in the revolution, but will become evident only in the new order which the revolution will bring about. This ploy has the merit of an element of honesty. There is no doubt that we are conditioned by the values of the present system which are loaded on behalf of the status quo: obedience, patience, patriotism, loyalty, etc. It is also honest to confess that being part of the revolution does not confer the status of gnostic, with all kinds of special insights reserved only for the initiated. Joining the revolution becomes then a matter of blind faith. The action that now seems wrong or absurd, it is asserted, will in the new order be vindicated as the course of right and wisdom. How do

I know? I don't, but I trust the revolution, historical necessity, and the logic of revolutionary force. For people in need of a faith, this kind of "revolutionary reasoning" may be highly satisfying. Revolutionary thought that is worthy of our attention, however, leads to a commitment made not in blind faith but clear vision, not based upon a sacrifice of intellect but motivated by an honest struggle with the problems and possibilities of the empirical situation.

The responsible revolutionary seeks no refuge in obscurantism. He may seem fanatical in the fervor of his commitment, but he is not a fanatic. He is more responsible than the protectors of the prevailing order who prattle endlessly about "responsibility." Whether he is a Bolivian peasant or an American professor, he exercises his full moral and intellectual capacity. As aware as he can be of the counterarguments and of the provisionality of his understanding, conscious of the possible consequences, open to the possibility that the future may prove him wrong, he decides for revolution. He is the responsible revolutionary.

On Not Doing Murder

"Thou shalt not kill" sounds unequivocal indeed. This is not the place to discuss the pacifist argument. The point is that most peoples have accepted certain social *justifications* for the taking of human life. Armed revolution assumes the taking of human life or at least the readiness to do so. In the Movement of recent years there has been general support for those who resist the draft and for those who desert, especially if it be for reasons of conscience, from the U.S. military. Opponents argued that "selective objection" undercut any conceivable social order since it left to individual decision what laws would be observed. The standard reply from the Movement is that a law that compels a man to kill another human being is qualitatively and self-evidently different from any other law. A society should not compel a person to do what is, in that person's view, murder.

Killing *is* qualitatively different. Every society has felt it necessary, however, to distinguish between killing and killing. We distinguish among murder, manslaughter, assassination, and killing in war, for instances. We distinguish between willful and accidental killing. The deliberate and socially legitimated killing in some societies, such as infanticide, head hunting, the killing of very old people, and cannibalism would be classified as murder in ours. There are even nuances distinguishing degrees of culpability in murder, thus we speak of murder in the first degree and so forth. Killing in one instance, in war for example, is considered heroic and in another is considered a crime. Neither are the society's sanctions equitably applied, as compare the treatment of a black man killing a policeman with the treatment of police who kill black men. Instances can be found in every major city. By one social system, that of the Third Reich, the ovens of Dachau were justified by reasons of social planning while in almost all others they are viewed as instruments of unspeakable crime.

In short, the very existence of a human community requires severe sanctions for the doing of murder. The revolutionary is by definition violating the code of the existing legal order. There are no legal revolutions. The revolutionary may say he appeals to a higher law than that framed by the society. Our job then is to understand what that higher law is. To say it is "revolutionary law" and therefore cannot be expressed in terms that are understandable outside the revolution or until the revolution is achieved is, as we have seen, evasive. This qualitatively different and solemn issue, the taking of human life, requires an adequate answer. The revolutionary may not hold himself answerable to the laws and prohibitions *of the present system.* But he knows he is answerable. The alternative is to be a murderer.

"The fact that a defendant acted pursuant to the order of his Government or of a superior shall not free him from responsibility." This principle of the Charter of the Nuremberg Tribunal has undergirded the radical war protest of the past few years. Actions from the Resistance to the several War Crime Tribunals have appealed to this principle in condemnation of the United States Government and vindication of the Movement. No doubt there are those who used Nuremberg for propaganda purposes but did not accept its philosophical premises about personal responsibility. I am convinced, however, that the consensus in the Movement is deeply committed to the moral obligation to resist illegitimate authority. The insight symbolized by Nuremberg has shaped the Movement and is one of the most wide-reaching developments shaping human consciousness in this era. If the revolution is to remain human, it too must be formed in respect, even reverence, for the insights emerging from the Nazi holocaust and articulated at Nuremberg.

We may paraphrase the principle: The fact that a defendant acted pursuant to the order of his revolutionary superiors (or the logic of history, or revolutionary necessity, etc.) shall not free him from responsibility. We are all in some sense "defendants." That is, we are accountable, whether we express it in terms of being accountable to God or to our own consciences or to the highest values known to us, or all these together. Most notably and singularly are we accountable for the taking of human life.

It is our purpose to suggest a framework for understanding "the just revolution." What are the circumstances that justify morally the exercise of man's right to revolution? In dealing with this question, no clear-cut answers will be supplied for every ethical problem that confronts the revolutionary. The focus is on the revolutionary enterprise as such. Under what circumstances does engagement in revolution make the taking of human life something other than murder? No claim of universal applicability is made for the answers proposed, and each person must wrestle with the questions in his own way. Finally he must internalize, make his own, whatever external criteria are suggested. Before the judgment of God and history each is responsible for his decision.

Again, the aim is not to encourage revolution. The express encouragement of armed revolution is of course illegal and one would be foolish to convict himself by writing a book of that nature. Some serious revolutionaries might challenge the value of even raising the question about the morality of revolution. Does it not have the effect of inhibiting revolutionary fervor? The important thing is to recruit for the cause, to persuade people of the revolutionary answers rather than confuse them with revolutionary questions. In response, I suggest that revolutionaries must themselves be fundamentally revolutionized. A revolutionary commitment that is the product of being temporarily overwhelmed by rhetoric or passion is not a reliable commitment. To the best of his ability, the revolutionary should understand and incorporate the revolutionary vision, examining it by bringing to bear upon it all the ideas, values and experiences that shape his view of the world. In this way, in the fullness and refinement of revolutionary consciousness, he makes the revolution his own, and is thus the more effective revolutionary. Of course, the result of his thorough examination may be that he decides not to be a revolutionary. Such are the risks of thinking.

To Justify the Offense

American society countenances several forms of killing. Poor people are killed by hunger or by the absence of medical care. Thousands are slaughtered regularly in rituals connected with the American cult of the automobile. Loneliness and the inability to succeed in a competitive society drive other thousands to suicide each year. In all these instances human life is taken. But it is difficult to locate responsibility. Certainly the indifference of those who have decision-making power is responsible for the deaths by malnutrition of sharecropper children in Mississippi. In the Illinois legislature there are those who could do something about medical care for the residents of Chicago's South Side. Executives in the extravagantly appointed offices of Ford Motor Company are clearly implicated. But no criminal charges arise from these deaths. When confronted with their causal roles, those in authority in each instance plead innocence. They claim they do not have the power to change the System, that the deaths are only a secondary, or accidental, consequence of their otherwise useful enterprise. "It is not our intention to kill anyone."

Intention is closely related to responsibility. True, a person is responsible for evil even if he does not intend the evil itself but does follow a course that increases the likelihood of evil, although the evil may be viewed as a side effect. Certainly one is responsible if by omission of doing good—not feeding the hungry, for instance—great evil results. In such instances our American society should much more rigorously call to account those who are responsible for the killings it tolerates so lightly. This is politically difficult, of course, because it involves people and practices in high places. Bringing the guilty to account also becomes, the more we think about it, morally slippery and legally elusive. "Some are guilty, all are responsible," says Rabbi Abraham Heschel. Complicity embraces the whole society. The best we can do, the reformers argue, is to provoke the public that is "responsible" to demand greater accountability from the decision-makers who are "guilty." But finally both conservatives and radicals tend to agree that it is the System itself that is to blame. The conservatives agree because, being sympathetic to the power elite, they do not wish to see punishment exacted. The radicals agree because they do not wish to see moral indignation against the System dissipated by the endless pursuit of guilty individuals. "The system itself must be restructured," is the radical creed.

The revolutionary prospect involves a different kind of killing. All killing and being killed is the same, of course, in its singular finality. But not all killing is the same in terms of its social uses and consequences. Unlike the killings mentioned above, some killing is deliberate and direct, publicly professed and socially approved. In American society the two chief instances of such killing are capital punishment and war. In these instances the person or persons who actually do the killing can confess the deed in public and will not be liable to legal action and may indeed be honored for their action. War in this connection includes also police actions in which life may be taken in the warfare between police and the presumably criminal elements of the society, the latter being literally outlaws in the sense that they are outside the protection of the law. In the revolutionary situation, revolutionaries are outlaws. On the other hand, in the revolutionary situation the protectors of the present order are outside the law of the revolution.

The kind of killing under discussion, then, is the killing that is deliberate, direct, professed, and sanctioned. Both the revolutionary and the agent of the state believe they are justified in such killing. Each seeks social vindication. The ethical dynamics are the same, both recognize the wrong of taking human life in an individualistic or arbitrary way. Both appeal to the judgment of the community. The difference is that they live in different communities of discourse. What makes a man a criminal in the eyes of the ruling regime makes him a hero in the eyes of his revolutionary fellows. Each community of discourse has its own version of reality and also a system of punishment and rewards to reinforce its world view. Both the state and the revolutionary party justify the taking of human life not, or at least not usually, as a good in itself but as a necessity warranted by the goal of maintaining, or acquiring, the power essential to support its version of reality.

The justification, however, goes beyond simple power seeking or power maintenance. To be sure, there was once a time when kings thought they ruled by divine right and therefore the maintenance of kingly power was a self-evidently adequate justification for any use of force. Such claims have little credibility today and no power elite attempts to make them, at least not in the western world. Governor Reagan does not attempt to justify the killing of a black youth in Oakland by saying that the insurgency there threatened his personal power. He appeals to ideas of public good, order, peace, and the like. He attempts to identify his power as an instrument of a higher good which claims the loyalty of the citizenry. In short, he seeks to associate his power with authority, for power without authority is only force, and force is not self-authenticating. It is not possible to appeal to force to justify the use of force. Likewise the revolutionary, unless he has completely blown his mind on the mystique of violence, appeals from force to power and, in turn, from power to the authority that legitimates the power and, consequently, warrants the force necessary to maintain the power.

The regime and the revolution exist in different communities of discourse, yet neither can be content to rest the case for its legitimation with that community of discourse alone. Each insists that there are "objective" points of reference by which its course is justified. Each must insist on this point, or else its presumed authority is arbitrary and subjective, even if it is a communal arbitrariness and subjectivity.

A persuasive justification must have in it a thrust toward the universal, toward a truth that transcends the partisanship of a particular viewpoint. The regime may appeal to a "divine order" and the revolutionary to "historical necessity," but the modern critical mind finds these appeals less than persuasive. Both the divine right of kings and historical messianism have been proved not only bankrupt but disastrous in their consequences. A case does not need to be made today against the divine right of kings, but it is not so clear to everyone that the argument from historical necessity has been refuted by history itself. That ought to be decisive, like God coming out against the theory of the divine right of kings, but there are still Marxists and would-be Marxists who are unconvinced.

The Higher Good and Human Life

Both revolution and regime must persuade their adherents that they are the instruments of a higher good. This "good" is spelled out in ways that make sense and seem desirable to the adherents and prospective adherents. The statement of the higher good should stand up under public scrutiny and criticism. Both revolution and regime will appeal to some of the same concepts and experiences in articulating the higher good: justice, peace, prosperity and, in some cases, self-determination. Each will try to demonstrate that there is an element of the universal in the higher good to which it is committed. The person who listens to the argument recognizes that these notions comprising the higher good remain unmistakably influenced by different worlds of discourse. "Justice" for Senator Eastland means the continued exploitation of his sharecropping black people; "peace" for Mayor Daley means crushing the skulls of demonstrators; "prosperity" for the trade union membership means exclusion of blacks and Puerto Ricans; and the United States' notion of "self-determination" implies counterrevolutionary repression around two thirds of the globe.

The recognition of subjectivity, both personal and in one's community of discourse, can easily lead to cynicism. The politically simple man who says, "The higher good be damned. What's in it for me?" has his counterpart in more sophisticated circles. The political effectiveness of cynicism is revealed in our society by the way in which serious political discussion is short-circuited by appeal to the material success of the Great American Way. In political debate, creature comforts are matched against moral and philosophical argument and, with discouraging consistency, the former carry the day. In an economically developed country such as the United States, the appeal to the belly and the pocketbook weights the argument in favor of the status quo, at least for the great majority of Americans. It is therefore more urgent and more difficult for the revolutionary to articulate a higher good by which this consumer society must be judged. Here we are discussing the values and conditions that may give moral legitimacy to armed revolution. But even if there is no such revolution, the growth of the discussion itself can enliven and illuminate the quality of public discourse in and about American life. Whether the United States needs armed revolution may be open to question, but this country desperately needs to confront the issues raised by revolutionary thought.

The idea of taking human life is prominent in these remarks about revolutionary violence, some may think the idea is given inordinate emphasis. I make no apology for that. In 1968 a campaign worker for Hubert Humphrey told me, "The trouble with you people who won't support Hubert is that you're hung up on Vietnam." I readily admitted to being hung up on Vietnam. Likewise, I admit to being hung up on human life. Recently in Mexico a North American college instructor declared, "A revolutionary has to get his priorities straight, and, for a revolutionary, human life has to be way down on the list of his priorities." This notion, too often heard in the rhetoric of those who aspire to the revolutionary style, should be categorically rejected. It is the linchpin of every despotism, whether of Right or Left, that has brutally violated man. It is both odious to the revolutionary humanist and unnecessary for the success of revolutions. At times it may be necessary to take particular human lives in order to achieve the purposes of the revolution. But those purposes themselves must finally be framed in terms of human life values if the revolution is to have any claim on those who believe there is no higher moral value than the cherishing and fulfillment of human life. The revolution must credibly assert that it cares more, not less, about human life than does the regime it opposes. The revolution's reason for being is the conviction that the cherishing and fulfillment of human life requires fundamental change in the social and political order. "Humanism" like "responsibility" is an idea that cannot be surrendered to the opposition.

Revolutionary humanism involves being concerned about more than the killing of human life. There are innumerable ways in which humanity is violated, and all of them are required for the success of armed revolution. Secrecy and deception must be skillfully refined by those who are outlaws in the eyes of the established order. The revolutionary must be prepared, for the sake of the revolution, to exploit friendships, betray personal trust, to tell lies. Especially in guerrilla warfare, the revolutionary should be ready to utilize torture, the most degrading and dehumanizing violation of humanity. In short, the revolutionary is prepared to act in specifics against all his most humane and compassionate instincts in order to achieve the higher good of the revolutionary purpose. The more the revolutionary is repulsed by the harsh necessities of revolution, the more essential it becomes for him to think through the humanizing rationale, the justification, of the revolution.

If the revolution is achieved at the price of his own humanity, the revolutionary becomes the most pathetic of figures. He may claim that he is prepared to sacrifice his own humanity for the sake of a new and more humanizing order, but the man who has lost his own humanity cannot bestow the gift of humanity on others. He can no longer distinguish between gift and curse, the living streams of compassion are dried up under the relentless heat of ideological fervor. This is the story of too many revolutions which, once established in power, resulted in new and more oppressive forms of tyranny.

The revolutionary is not alone in facing the danger of the loss of his humanity. The revolutionary's danger is not qualitatively different from that faced by the servants of the present repressive order. The Green Beret who in a "dirty war" obeys orders to torture and commit other outrages against his humane sensibilities tends to lose his sensibilities. He too appeals for justification to noble purposes such as "defending freedom," but the more he is involved in this version of freedom's defense the less probable it is that he can understand the meaning of the "freedom" for which he destroys himself. Similar dynamics are present in the industrialist's greed and the politician's indifference. In perpetuating injustice they see themselves as instruments of a higher good, the American Way, the free enterprise system, or whatever. Their perception of the ends is clouded by preoccupation with the means. Words such as freedom and democracy are little more than verbal anesthetics to ease their guilty consciences. They speak the language of human values but do not understand it.

No man, whether revolutionary or defender of the old regime, is morally invincible. Anyone who is inclined to forget or belittle this fact is dangerous to his fellows, no matter how noble the goals he professes. Each group seeks to articulate a justifying rationale for its actions, especially for those actions—killing, terrorism, torture, deception—offensive to humane sensibilities. In the next section we will look at some of the criteria by which such a justifying rationale might be constructed for armed revolution. The criteria suggested are not a set of absolute

principles absolutely applied. They are tentative, sugges-
tive, and relative. Using the same criteria, different readers
may come to different conclusions about the "rightness"
of armed revolution. At best they pose some of the
questions that should be worked through by anyone engaged, or considering engagement, in programmatic violence for the achievement of political and social ends.
If what follows only poses some questions and points
the direction to some answers, it will have achieved its
purpose for revolutionaries who are sensitive to the fragility of human community and of their own humanity.
Only in this way can we further a revolutionary humanism claiming the loyalties of honorable men.

War and Revolution

There are great differences between revolution and war.
War involves conflict between sovereign states. War is
waged between distinguishable political and social entities,
each with its own territory, and is very often sparked by
disputes about aggrandizing or defending territory. War
is inter-national. In revolution, on the other hand, sovereignty is up for grabs within a specific political and
social entity. Territorial lines are incidental in a revolution.
(The U. S. Civil War and the Biafran-Nigerian conflict
are not really revolutions but wars of secession.) Revolution is intra-national. This is true even of the thrust
of the former Communist Internationale which envisioned
success through the spread and co-ordination of intra-
national class conflict. In spite, however, of these and
other differences between war and revolution, there are
some striking similarities.

Both war and revolution resort to force for political
and social purposes. The purpose may be to initiate the

new revolutionary order or to protect the old order. In both cases the use of force is "justified" by appeal to politics and, as we have seen, to a legitimating authority supporting a political option. It is not surprising, therefore, that a history of thought has developed regarding the justification of resort to violence. The ability of a political order to maintain or achieve dominance depends largely upon the credibility of its supporting vision. "Where there is no vision," warned the biblical prophet, "the people perish." A compelling vision is needed to motivate people to die in defense of the old order or in pursuit of the new. The political purpose that cannot enlist radical self-sacrifice likely has little future. It is therefore worth our while to consider the way people have justified the resort to force for political and social purposes, war being the most common instance of such resort. We can then try to apply what we learn to the modern revolutionary moment.

Morally sensitive men have responded to the problem of war and violence in essentially three ways. *Pacifism* rejects absolutely the use of violence to resolve human problems. The *crusader* surrenders himself uncritically to the cause in which he is engaged and the violence it requires. Most others take a *discriminatory* approach to war, distinguishing among conflicts as to their rightness or wrongness, justice or injustice. There are important nuances within each of these positions which space does not permit us to discuss. The three-part distinction remains valid in our day.

It is obvious from previous remarks that the pacifist position, whether strategic, ideological or both, is a very lively option. For the purposes of this discussion of armed revolution, however, we set that option aside. The crusader option has been excluded by history as it requires religious and philosophical props of absolutism which have been rightly discredited since the Enlightenment. It is true that General Eisenhower entitled his memoirs of

World War II *Crusade in Europe* and the patriots of the "My country right or wrong" mentality are still much with us. But the crusade as the cause of absolute righteousness which can demand the suspension of all critical faculties remains a live option only for the mindless and for the fanatic who needs a faith to liberate him from the burden of uncertainty. The revolutionary who has not lost his humanity distinguishes among actual and potential conflicts. Which is just and which unjust? What ends can justify means that, under ordinary circumstances, are reprehensible? The mature revolutionary knows that, contrary to the ethical bromide, ends do justify means.

The end does not, however, justify any means. There are, according to the modern mind, "crimes against humanity" that no good end can justify. This suggests that, although we cannot specify in history any absolute good, we can specify instances of absolute evil. Neither does the notion that ends justify means intend to suggest that evil means are made good. Evil remains evil. To justify the doing of an evil thing does not mean that the thing itself is transformed. It does mean that it may be right to do a wrong thing in order to achieve a goal that is greater in good than the thing done is great in evil. The classic example, of course, is the poor man's stealing of a loaf of bread in order to feed his starving family.

Some enthusiasts presently auditioning for the revolution talk about the "amorality" of the revolution, or about "revolutionary ethics" or about "the ethical reversal" required for revolutionary action. There is nothing wrong with dressing things up in new jargon, so long as we understand that we are wrestling with the same question that preoccupied Socrates, Jesus, Augustine, Aquinas, and reflective men of our own time. Warfare brings to a head the questions that agonize men who believe that, in the ambiguity of the human condition, they must choose not so much between good and evil as among several evils. Their personal integrity rests on the hope that they choose the lesser evils for the sake of the good.

The Measure of Justice

The definition of a "just war" does not come to us in a unified form. Bits and pieces of the definition derive from different religious and ethical thinkers of different time and circumstance. The definition is susceptible to interpretation and abuse. There has never been a warring party that did not claim its cause to be just. If individuals or countries are determined to fight there is no limit to man's imaginative capacity to devise rationalizations for the course chosen, no matter how abhorrent it may seem to others. Nevertheless, the effort to define a just war is important simply because it implicitly rejects crusading fanaticism. It is an acknowledgment that no cause is self-authenticating, self-evidently right. The definition is further important because it supplies a framework, points of reference, by which thoughtful men can evaluate a course of action.

The definition of a just war, as we shall discuss it here, has seven parts. A just war is a war: (1) that is declared by legitimate public authority; (2) that is in response to a real injury that has been suffered; (3) that is undertaken only after all reasonable means of peaceful settlement have been exhausted; (4) in which those prosecuting the war have good intention; (5) in which damage likely to be incurred by the war will not be disproportionate to the injury suffered; (6) that employs only legitimate and moral means; (7) in which there is reasonable hope for success.

This definition may seem terribly academic, far removed from the passions of Harlem's 125th Street and the seizure of campus buildings. Yet, carefully explored, it touches on almost every aspect of today's revolutionary thought and action. Certainly it has been pointedly relevant to the non-pacifist protest against the Vietnam war, a war that, I believe, is condemned as unjust on all seven counts. This definition or an approximation of it is at the heart of the argument offered by "selective conscientious objectors." In various forms these seven points of reference constitute the claim of the Resistance to moral authority.

The definition will prove equally useful as a framework for our thinking about the ethics of revolution. Again, we are thinking about revolution in general—in Guatemala, South Africa, Thailand, Argentina, and two dozen other places where determined patriots conspire to break the chains of slavery. It is hoped that the questions and criteria suggested have a degree of general applicability, if not of universality. But in all that follows we have in mind particularly our own country. The drift is ending, questions long repressed now emerge, we confront the prospect of the next American Revolution.

Revolution by Legitimate Authority

"A just revolution is a revolution declared by legitimate public authority." This first criteria of a "just war" seems patently irrelevant to a "just revolution." No established government makes a revolution against itself. Of course governments declare "revolutionary" new programs in the spheres of economics, politics and social welfare. President Nixon publicly claims his program of family income maintenance, for instance, is "revolutionary." But this is so much verbiage intended to solidify rather than overthrow the power of the present order. It is not true, as some of our leftist colleagues claim, that a government never surrenders power. But even when a government surrenders or shares certain aspects of power, it is motivated by the necessity of circumstances in the hope that by compromise greater stability may be achieved under the prevailing regime. The point is, if real revolution had to await declaration by "legitimate public authority," there would be no revolution.

Even this first criterion of a just war is applicable to revolution, however. The serious revolutionary sees the need for authoritative direction. The alternative is chaos. In the present phase of revolutionary consciousness in America, revolutionaries frequently declare themselves in favor of chaos. Confusion and chaos, however, are temporary values, necessary to expose the brutal clumsiness of the present regime and to undermine popular confidence in it. The next revolutionary phase requires positing a credible revolutionary alternative to the regime. This, in turn, requires a clear notion of "legitimate authority" within the revolution itself. In short, "revolution for the hell of it" is only a preliminary to "revolution for a new order."

Before the legitimate revolutionary authority can be recognized the legitimate authority of the regime must be discredited. It is said frequently by radicals today that the System has been delegitimized. As an individual statement of attitude, this presents no great problems. It means that a person or group of persons find the present regime to be unsupported by, indeed in conflict with, those values that lend moral authority to institutional behavior. The problem is to transfer such individual value judgments into political practice.

Every regime takes steps to discourage, and if possible to preclude, the process by which it can be delegitimized in the popular mind. Fascism of the German and Italian variety made the most thorough effort in this direction. An ideology was developed and propagated which excluded all transcendent points of reference. All legitimate "values" were incorporated into, and inseparable from, the regime itself. Therefore, according to the ideology of the Third Reich, there was no political-ethical framework beyond the Reich itself by which the Reich could be evaluated and brought under judgment. Communism of the Soviet variety is more ambivalent, less thorough. Marxist ideology based its claims to truth upon history. Theoretically, the truth or falsehood of Marxism will be manifest in historical events leading to and following the revolution of the proletariat. When the expectation of the withering away of the state, for example, is discredited by subsequent events, Marxist theory is in trouble. Because Marxist ideology makes itself vulnerable to history, the regime in the Soviet Union must increasingly revise its ideology to justify policies indistinguishable from those of fascism. Criticism must be severely repressed lest thoughtful people point out that history has stripped the Central Committee of its clothes. Only in this way can the regime hope to prevent its delegitimation.

Democracy of the U.S. variety also has its defenses against delegitimation. There is of course physical repression of criticism by police and military force. There are also more refined forms of legal repression. But overt repression is uncharacteristic of democracy, which is not the same as saying that overt repression is infrequent. Indeed in a democracy the use of overt repression tends to be self-defeating for the government and strengthens the case for delegitimation. The reaction of police and political forces to demonstrations at the 1968 Chicago Democratic Convention is an excellent case in point, marking a major success for those who would delegitimize the U.S. government. The more characteristic, and infinitely more subtle, style of democratic governments is to promote a repressive false consciousness which can preclude the criticism that leads to delegitimation.

The heart of a democratic false consciousness is in the phrase "government by the people, of the people and for the people." On the one hand, this is a compellingly noble concept, setting forth the thesis of participatory democracy. On the other, it is susceptible to being used as the most frustratingly clever form of repression. In its common and abusive form, it perpetuates the false consciousness that there really is no government at all. We are all the government, therefore we are not governed. It distracts popular attention from the small groups within the society who actually make the decisions and wield the power. That is, it distracts attention from the de facto government in the society. Political responsibility is dissipated; everyone is responsible, therefore no one is responsible. The government cannot be held to account by the people for, presumably, the government is the people.

As an expression of hope, "government by the people, of the people and for the people" is a noble sentiment. That is perhaps the way things will be in the Second Coming. But when used as a description of existing fact in our present history, the phrase is a dangerous lie. It is dangerous because it suggests the government is coextensive with the society. It is dangerous because it destroys the tension between the government and the governed. To the degree that people are deluded by this democratic false consciousness, they are as politically enslaved as the victims of the Third Reich, for they lack access to the transcendent points of reference by which the regime can be brought to judgment.

Americans are not accustomed to thinking of government as a regime. This is an unfortunate consequence of democratic false consciousness. Regime is not necessarily a derogatory term. It means simply the group that actually rules and manages affairs in a society. It is what C. Wright Mills called the power elite. Whether or not one agrees that the power elite is as closed and small a group as Mills suggests, the power elite is the regime. It is the *actual* power-wielding group in the society, including not only—not even primarily—those who are publicly recognized because they hold office through electoral politics, but also, for example, the leadership of the military-industrial-university complex. The regime may be monolithic or diverse, large or small, responsive to public need or capricious, progressive or reactionary, but it remains the regime. Revolution requires a clear understanding of who "they" are who constitute the regime. Legitimate authority within the revolution implies the delegitimation of the regime. And the regime cannot be delegitimized until it has been identified.

It is therefore neither accurate nor strategically helpful to declare revolution against an undifferentiated System or against "the captivity of the American Way of Life," or against "white America" as such. In fact these generalized declarations of war are self-defeating for the revolution. They fall into the obverse trap of the democratic false consciousness. That is, they reinforce the myth that the regime is coextensive with the society and thereby everyone is put on the defensive and will, in understandable alarm, rush to support the regime's legitimacy. The consequence of such revolutionary blundering is evident in today's overwhelmingly popular support for "law and order." Again, in order to delegitimize the regime, it must be identified in such a way that the popular mind is able to make the distinction between the interests of the people and the interests of the regime that is under attack. More simply, the revolution must be seen as being against the regime but for the people.

The question of legitimacy is closely linked to the notion of sovereignty. In modern democratic thought it is supposed that the people are sovereign and that the government is an instrument of the people's will. Revolution, in the minds of America's more radical founders, was both right and necessary when the pretensions of the government threatened the sovereignty of the people. A revolution thus undertaken would be "by legitimate public authority." There have been instances in American life where the will of the "sovereign" people has been clearly frustrated by the regime. In the nineteenth century, Stephen A. Douglas' doctrine of "popular sovereignty" by which the residents of a territory were to be free to decide for or against slavery was overthrown by the Supreme Court.

In 1968, millions of Americans believed the party system of electoral politics frustrated the will of the people for dramatic change from Lyndon Johnson's course in Vietnam. These are two instances in which the will of the legitimate authority, the people, was right and the regime was wrong but triumphant.

There are other instances in which the contrary was the case, in which the popular will was wrong and the government right. There is little doubt that during the early 1950s the great majority of Americans were in basic agreement with Joseph McCarthy's anti-Communist crusade, but the will of the sovereign people was frustrated by the regime's constitutional constraints. Similarly, the FBI's repression of the Black Panthers and others (J. Edgar Hoover calls the Panthers "the most dangerous subversive group in America today") is no doubt supported by popular mandate. Indeed, in the area of civil liberties generally, whatever restraints have been imposed upon police power have come from within the government itself (especially from the judiciary) rather than from the sovereign people.

These observations are not made in praise of America's governmental system. Every politically literate citizen knows how empty is much of the boasting found in high school civics textbooks. The purpose of these observations is rather to refine our notion of legitimate authority, and to understand the circumstances in which that authority calls for revolution. Consider a circumstance from the past, the Dred Scott decision of the Supreme Court, in 1857. A regime cannot claim authority from the sovereignty of the people if that regime explicitly excludes people from participation. The Dred Scott decision declared that black people were not citizens and therefore could not sue in the federal courts nor participate in any other public business appropriate to citizenship. At least at that point in American history, all slaves were made outlaws. That is, as persons rather than as property, black people were put outside the law of the prevailing order. The sovereignty residing in the black people was not only threatened but absolutely denied by the regime. The right to black revolution by legitimate authority was therefore unquestionable. Of course, with the exception of Nat Turner and a few others, the regime successfully and cruelly prevented the exercise of the right to revolution.

A similar claim to the right to revolution is implicit in the "basic definition" of the Black Panther Party:

> We start with the basic definition: that black people in America are a colonized people in every sense of the term and that white America is an organized Imperialist force holding black people in colonial bondage.

If this statement is accurate, and if we accept the democratic notion that sovereignty resides in the people, the Black Panther "basic definition" lays a clear foundation for the right to black revolution by legitimate authority.

All regimes are imperfect, some are more imperfect than others. Every regime in various ways is unresponsive to the sovereign people or to large sectors of the people. At what point does a regime's opposition to the legitimate authority of the people become explicit, consistent and a matter of policy rather than of remediable error? At whatever point that is, that is the point at which the illegitimate authority of the regime must be opposed by the legitimate authority of the people.

When that point is reached and a revolutionary situation prevails, we face the same question in a different form. Assuming that the revolution is declared in the name of the sovereign people, who within the revolution speaks for the people? It is quite possible that within the revolution itself a regime, a ruling group, may emerge that is as illegitimate in authority as is the regime against which the revolution is declared. Obviously, "the people" is not one person and one voice but a heterogeneous crowd of individuals making cacophonous noises. Where then is legitimacy to be found?

It might be suggested that the revolution should transcend nationalism and that, therefore, we should not be distracted by the problem of trying to ascertain the will of the people in the particular society in which the revolution is declared. That means that, if the revolution is declared in the United States, it is declared "in the name of the suffering peoples of the Third World," or in the "name of humanity." As attractive as such language is, it is also evasive. If it is difficult to locate the voice of "the people" of this one society, it is infinitely more difficult to locate the voice of the billions outside this society. "The wretched of the earth" is an important and compelling metaphor, but it should not be confused with a political entity capable of exercising rights and bestowing legitimacy. Leadership that acts "in the name of humanity" is leadership that wants to escape accountability. Men and their communities, not humanity in general, bring leadership to judgment. Leadership that cannot be brought to judgment receives its mandate only from the gun and/or the manipulation of mobs.

Jean-Jacques Rousseau (1712–78) wrestled with this problem we have here and developed a sophisticated notion of "the general will" of the people. A legitimate government is a government responsive to the "general will." Unfortunately, this notion did not fare too well after the French Revolution. Because the "general will" could not be *identified* with the will of any specific individuals or groups it soon became the case that a policy was thought not to reflect the "general will" if it *coincided* with the wishes of any individual or group. As Hannah Arendt points out in *On Revolution,* the failure of the French Revolution was in large part caused by an apotheosized notion of the "general will" that denied the sovereignty of the actual people on whose behalf the "general will" was presumably exercised.

Herbert Marcuse in his *One-Dimensional Man* helps us to cut the Gordian knot in determining the relation-

ship between "the people" and the legitimate authority
and leadership of the "just revolution":

> To the degree to which the slaves [the general populace
> under repressive capitalism] have been preconditioned to
> exist as slaves and be content in that role, their liberation
> necessarily appears to come from without and from above.
> They must be "forced to be free," to "see objects as they
> are, and sometimes as they ought to appear," they must be
> shown the "good road" they are in search of. But with
> all its truth, the argument cannot answer the time-honored
> question: who educates the educators, and where is the
> proof that they are in possession of "the good"?

Marcuse goes on to argue for an "educational dictatorship"
on the grounds that the terrible risk involved may not
be more terrible "than the risk which the great liberal as
well as the authoritarian societies are taking now, nor may
the costs be much higher." Marcuse's is a frankly elitist
argument in the Marxist tradition. Because the people
are not free, legitimate authority rests with the revolution
that does not *reflect* the people's present will but rather
anticipates what the will of the people will be when they
are freed by the revolution. The "enlightened" revolutionaries educate the people to what the people desire,
even though, because they are slaves, the people may
suffer from the delusion that they desire quite the opposite.
It is apparent, according to this theory, that what the
will of the people will be in the new order is the true,
although hidden, will of the people now.

If the reader finds himself confused by the circular
argumentation and metaphysical nuances of the above remarks, he may take comfort in knowing he is in the
company of most Marxist thinkers of our time. While
we may not agree with his answers, Marcuse's statement
is extremely helpful in clarifying two issues: first, revolutions are declared and led not by the people in general
but by a revolutionary elite; second, the revolution's
justification is inseparable from the future that is its
goal. It is the first issue that concerns us immediately.

It is commonly said that revolutions are made by three per cent of the population. As useful as this observation is, it must also be pointed out that a population is composed of a number of "three per cents." Elitist definitions are extremely slippery. The "Five Percenters" in New York's black community claim that eighty-five per cent of the black people are cows, ten per cent have sold out to white America, and five per cent understand what is happening and can do something about it. Confusingly enough, however, the "Five Percenters" are in frequent conflict with the "three per cent" that is making revolution. The point is not to ridicule this situation but to illustrate that hard decisions must be made by those who engage in revolution. As long as revolution is simply radical talk, it is enough to identify with everyone who shares in the revolutionary consciousness of the Movement. When revolution gets serious, however, it is necessary to determine which leadership represents the direction and authority of a just revolution.

Revolutionary leadership almost inevitably tends toward the dictatorial. The more intense the conflict between revolution and regime, the less possibility there is of popular sharing in decision-making. Halting operations in order to renew the leadership mandate through elections or other democratic procedures imperils the whole revolutionary enterprise. Some decisions about leadership should be made before the shooting begins, if we are to avoid the tragedy described by Richard Barnet in *Intervention and Revolution:*

> The revolutionary, even when he is fired by a righteous cause, often marks his success by reverting to the political type he supplants. He becomes a political intriguer, a persecutor of critics, a lover of luxury, or an addict of personal adulation.

Of course there is no guaranteed leadership formula to prevent the perversion of the revolution. But before the revolutionary pledges his "life, fortune and sacred honor" to the cause, he will want to be reasonably confident that the revolution itself will not be delegitimized by internecine conflict and corruption. Some revolutions, such as that in Cuba with Fidel Castro, begin with charismatic leadership that is able to provide continuity of intention and to claim the confidence of supporters. Lacking such leadership, revolutions become vulnerable to having their intention radically distorted. The take-over of the Russian Revolution by Lenin and his Bolsheviks is a dramatic case in point.

In the first American Revolution, there was extensive and vigorous debate long before the revolution got underway about how power would be distributed and decisions made. It is said that John Adams collected constitutions the way other people collect stamps. Pre-revolutionary conferences and proposals hardly answered all the questions that might come up, but they assured that the revolution would not be surprised, captured or overwhelmed in the moment of its success. To be sure, the circumstances prevailing in eighteenth-century America are not comparable to any revolutionary or pre-revolutionary situations of our day. The effort to anticipate the course and outcome of revolutionary action, however, is equally imperative. It might be argued that, given the rapidity of events in modern situations of conflict, such anticipation is doubly necessary.

Some advocates of revolution contend that revolutionary passion should not be inhibited by too much concern for the future. "The important thing is not to think but to act!" "There is no sense in trying to split up the pie before power has been achieved." Such statements as these are more appropriate to a gang of bandits planning a job than they are to revolutionaries determined to transform society. If anticipating the future means deciding how to divide the loot, then not only such planning but the revolution itself is unworthy of further attention. The important question at hand is not one of distributing the spoils but of providing reasonable assurance that the revolution will, in its several phases, continue to operate by the legitimate authority of the sovereign people.

There are three types who discourage discussion about decision-making within the revolution: the naïve who are oblivious to the dangers of the revolution being distorted or captured; those who presently hold decision-making power and feel threatened by any discussion of the subject; those who hope to capture the revolution for purposes that the majority of revolutionaries are "not yet ready" to understand or accept. The first type is hopelessly innocent. The other two, while they may include men of admirable intentions, are structurally oriented to betraying the revolution, since they evade accountability to the sovereign authority that alone can make and keep the revolution legitimate.

I have mentioned the role of charismatic leadership in the revolution. "Charismatic" is, of course, a term so overused that it has been robbed of much of its meaning. Anyone for whom the media can contrive a reasonably attractive image is called charismatic. It is conceivable that by 1972 even the bumptious banalities of Hubert Humphrey will be described as evidences of charismatic leadership. With TV politics, as with God, all things are possible. The Greek word *charisma*, however, means a special grace. The charismatic leader is a personal moment of grace in history, a man uncontrived who embodies in his person the values and strengths that claim the loyalties of lesser men. The charismatic revolutionary leader is the one who bears within himself, and is able to communicate to others, the "spirit" of the revolution. The devotion he inspires is different from hero-worship because it distinguishes between the leader himself and the values which he bears. In actual consequences, however, charismatic leadership and hero-worship are often indistinguishable. When the distinction between the man and the values is obliterated or seriously weakened, the "heroic leader" almost inevitably becomes the tyrant of the revolution that fails in its success.

If the revolution is to remain legitimate, the most charismatic leadership must be held accountable to the revolution. One of the roles of ideology is to keep personal leadership in check. Ho Chi Minh, unquestionably a charismatic leader, called men not to follow him personally but to commit themselves to the goals of the new revolutionary order that had been refined through decades of reflection and debate. The wedding of charismatic leadership and ideology has proved essential in most revolutions. The leadership most frequently appealed to by revolutionaries in the United States is dead. At present the revolution has a list of saints but few leaders. The ideology has, presumably, been conceived, diverse and often contradictory seeds being deposited with passionate regularity. Attempts to rush the gestation period will result in the abortion that is commonly described as the fragmentation of the Left.

The "Manifesto" of the Black Economic Development Conference asserts that the leadership of the revolution must be completely black. A remarkable number of white radicals seem prepared to accept this premise. While it is likely, for the reasons discussed earlier, that charismatic leadership for radical change in America will emerge from the black rather than the white population, this is not the same thing as accepting the premise of black revolutionary leadership. White radicals who subscribe to the chauvinism of black moral superiority are probably more involved in working out their guilt feelings and need for political mythology than in serious thinking about the legitimacy of the revolution.

The myth of "the black man," like that of "the people," is a powerful metaphor, but only a metaphor. To assume that there is a politicially locatable thing called "the black man" is an insult to the rich diversity to be discovered among black brothers. The problem of revolutionary leadership is not resolved by limiting the search for leadership to the black community. Such a limitation excludes the sovereignty residing in the majority of the

American people for whom we are supposedly making the revolution. Also, such a limitation denies the dignity of black people by refusing to recognize that black people have not only the capacity for good but also the capacity for evil equal to that possessed by other people.

There is an evident condescension in some white radical willingness to follow black leadership. White leadership is held to account, with reasons demanded for each decision. If the same demands are not made of black leadership, it is not necessarily because black leadership is more trusted but because too many white radicals subconsciously assume that blacks are incapable of rendering account. Solid revolutionary alliances are built on mutual respect, and respect demands that each partner, black and white, challenge the other to meet his own highest standard of thought and commitment.

In summary, the first criterion of a just war, that it be declared by legitimate public authority, seems to be inapplicable to determining what is a just revolution, until we understand that the legitimate public authority is the authority of the sovereign people. In order to conceive of a revolution by legitimate authority it was necessary to discuss the circumstances that delegitimize the prevailing regime. Since revolutions are not declared by consensus or majority vote but by a revolutionary elite, the problem of leadership within the revolution is inescapable. The leadership problem has to do not primarily with effectiveness but with maintaining the legitimate authority by which the revolution is undertaken. The crucial question is this: How can it be reasonably assured that the revolutionary elite, which by definition is not *of* and *by* the people, will remain *for* the people in a way that does not betray the authority it claims *from* the people.

Throughout this discussion we have assumed that "the people" is the source of public authority. That is, while the revolution may be committed to more absolute values such as Justice, Liberty, Honor, and Truth, these values are not separable from "the people" who alone can legitimately mandate the implementation of these values in public life. This assumption is quite frankly a democratic prejudice. Beginning from some other assumption— the logic of history, a mandate from God et al.—the discussion of legitimate authority would take a quite different direction. Wherever one begins, however, the question of legitimate authority is crucial to the idea of a just revolution. The alternative is moral nihilism which, unless counteracted, will surely destroy the revolution it invites.

Given the state of the leadership, base of support and ideology, I am persuaded that American radicalism cannot presently meet this first criterion of a just revolution. At the summer 1969 Oakland meeting of the United Front Against Fascism, Bobby Seale of the Black Panther Party, emphasized that American revolutionaries are just beginning to take a few preliminary steps toward revolutionary alliance. It was said that it may take fifty or a hundred years to build a revolutionary movement in the United States. This, I believe, is a realistic estimate that should be accepted by all who do not want revolution for the hell of it but revolution by legitimate authority.

Revolution in Response to Injury

Nobody wants war. Ask any general. Each party to a conflict laments the conditions that forced war upon them. Hitler moves into Poland, the Soviet Union into Czechoslovakia, and the U.S. into Vietnam, all "in response to real injury." The regime that is set on war has little difficulty in contriving the incidents required for the formality of justice. In 1964 the alleged attack by the North Vietnamese on U.S. vessels in the Tonkin Gulf "justified" U.S. bombardment of North Vietnam. The incident, it has been subsequently demonstrated, was largely contrived, but it admirably achieved its purpose by getting from the Senate a resolution that the Johnson Administration was later to interpret as being tantamount to a declaration of war.

The second measurement of a just war, that it must be in response to real injury suffered, is leveled at the conventional deceits practiced by nations. Seldom, if ever, does a regime declare it is going to war in order to secure better markets, to aggrandize its territory, or simply because it is spoiling for a good fight. Nobody knows better than the military that war is hell, and therefore undertaken as painful necessity.

> I have offered the enemy my hand again and again . . . We have never demanded anything from them we have never insisted on anything . . . We have been drawn into war against our will. No man can offer his hand more often than I have. But if they want to exterminate us then they will get the surprise of their lives.

Thus Adolf Hitler, shortly before Stalingrad, assured the German people that his course was "in response to real injury suffered."

Revolutionaries also declare war on the regime "in response to real injury suffered." Revolutionaries also can deceive themselves and their followers. The revolutionary, it may seem, is not as likely to contrive the appearance of injury. He does not have as much to gain by going to war. Unlike the militarist, he is not viewed as a hero but as an outlaw. He is not backed up by the "war effort" of the society, and when the fighting gets hot he is more likely to be injured or killed. Win or lose, the soldier can go back to his pursuits after the treaty is signed. For the revolutionary, the alternative to winning is execution or long imprisonment. The revolutionary, it would seem, should not seek excuses for warring against the regime. Nevertheless, revolutionaries can and do contrive occasions for war. The mystique of violence and vying for a place in the annals of revolutionary glory are not that different, psychologically from the dynamics that move the war machine of nations. A revolution may be judged unjust by this second measurement too.

"In response to real injury suffered" is a criterion so vague as to seem almost useless. But anyone who acknowledges the right to revolution and is even slightly acquainted with the tyrannies of our times will grant that this condition of a just revolution probably exists in some places. Rapacious dynasties extort the sweat and money of the masses so a few can live in splendor. Regimes devise racial laws explicitly aimed at excluding the black majority from political participation and personal freedom. Colonial powers, working through puppet regimes, imprison or execute indigenous leadership that threatens their exploitative hold over the territory of others. Even the strictest application of this second measurement suggests that the right to revolution may be rightfully exercised in such places as South Africa, Angola, Rhodesia, Spain, Guatemala, Haiti, Czechoslovakia, Hungary, Brazil, and, I believe, South Vietnam. This is a partial list, and, of course, we are here speaking of only one measurement of a just revolution. This does not mean that there should be revolution in any or all of these places but simply that revolution would be justified by the "real injury suffered" criterion.

One person's real injury is another person's minor inconvenience. The majority in any country would consider no real injury had been done if it were prohibited from publishing political opinions that differed with the party line of the regime. Most people do not publish political opinions. One person's equal opportunity is another's real injury. A blue-collar worker in the Ridgewood section of Queens considers it a very real and major injury if his children are bused to a largely black school in Brooklyn. Not only do people have quite different values that might be violated, people also have different "revolting levels." Public officials are accustomed to talking about "acceptable" levels of unemployment without consulting those who are without work, especially young blacks whose unemployment rates are three or four times the national average. Even more remarkable is the language about acceptable levels of fatalities in the case of nuclear war. The question that goes begging is, Acceptable to whom?

People in power generally have a higher "revolting level" than the powerless, since they are less immediately affected by society's injustices. At least that is the assumption of most popular revolutionary argument. The assumption is challenged, however, by Oscar Lewis and others who have described the "culture of poverty" in which the poor, the most immediate victims of injustice, are too depressed to take seriously the grand notions required for revolutionary action. My nine years of life and work with the black and Puerto Rican poor of New York City tends to confirm this analysis. The aspirations of the poor, far from aiming at a new world order, are distressingly bourgeois. A color TV, a new car, the children in a private school and a house with a yard to play in—these goals have little relation to a call to the barricades. Plans for revolution should not be immune to present facts, among which is the fact that, according to Harris polls, black Americans want to send their children to integrated schools (78 per cent to 9 per cent), live in integrated neighborhoods (74 to 16) and work in integrated job situations (82 to 11). Black Americans also believe (63 to 21) that these distinctly non-revolutionary goals can be achieved without violence. Those who believe violence is necessary or inevitable see it, for the most part, as a method of pressuring the System into working better, not as a revolutionary strategy for overthrowing the prevailing regime.

Who, then, determines the "real injury suffered"? Whose "revolting level" is crucial to deciding the justness of the revolution? Here again, as in our discussion of "legitimate authority," we see that revolution is an elitist enterprise. Several studies have confirmed that the revolutionary consciousness in America today is provoked and sustained not by the poor but by the middle and upper-middle-class youth who have seen through the Great American Way. The black leadership is also, for the most part, manifesting the most revolutionary thrust among the non-poor blacks. Stokely Carmichael is a commonly cited example. James Forman's wife is the daughter of Jessica Mitford, which gives him access to money and opportunity far beyond the dreams of most oppressed black Americans. Only the most superficial critic claims that these "advantages" disqualify such men from revolutionary leadership. It is rather to their credit that they have refused to play it safe and have identified with the disinherited.

The point to be made here, however, is that we should not be deceived by the conventional rhetoric that assumes revolution will arise from spontaneous combustion among the poor. The "revolting level" of the really poor is depressingly high. The revolutionary elite is very often also the economic and social elite. Revolution is made on behalf of the poor by those who are better prepared to understand the "real injury suffered." To many radicals this may sound terribly patronizing, precisely that kind of condescension they so vigorously condemn when it is practiced by liberals. The opposite of patronizing the poor, however, is not to pretend that all men are equal in influence, understanding, or opportunity. There are insights that the poor have, "soul" if you will, to which the rich are blind. Only by learning from the poor can the advantaged understand how disadvantaged they are in their comprehension of some of life's realities. But the radical's romanticizing of the life values possessed by the poor is as bad as any oppressor's fatuous claim that he envies the oppressed. The mystique of the poor, especially the poor black, that is dominant in some white radical circles is only the other side of the southern plantation owner's declaration about how happy his niggers are.

A solid revolutionary analysis requires a sense of history and of politico-economic dynamics that is not ordinarily possessed by the poor and uneducated. This does not mean the revolutionary elite is patronizing toward the poor, the effective elite works in genuine compassion with the poor, remembering that com-passion means suffering-with. The revolutionary does not win the confidence of the poor by pretending to be like them in all respects, but by throwing in his lot with the oppressed, by making himself vulnerable with them to the consequences of revolutionary actions undertaken on their behalf. No matter how much the economically privileged revolutionary may wish to identify with the poor, he cannot really become poor. Unlike the poor with whom he may throw in his lot he has options beyond poverty.

The revolutionary's credibility among the poor depends not upon his skill in "playing poor" but upon the confidence he inspires in the poor that he has voluntarily closed off his other options. This confidence is most severely tested when, for reasons of revolutionary strategy, the non-poor revolutionary may utilize his influence with the ruling class to obtain money or other requirements of the revolutionary movement. The oppressed are rightly suspicious of those who, claiming the best revolutionary intentions, move too readily between the camps. This is one of the continuing tensions between the revolution and its leadership.

The revolutionary elite, then, determines what is the "real injury suffered" that justifies making revolution. If the revolutionary begins with an impossibly beautiful vision of man and his communities, then there is no place on earth where revolution is not justified. That is, no social order is equal to the vision. Not only Angola and Guatemala but also Cuba and China are in need of revolution, because in none of these societies is want eliminated and man's hope for freedom and fulfillment completely satisfied. It is precisely this insight that leads some revolutionaries to call for "permanent revolution," and we shall look at this idea more closely when we come to discuss the "ends" and end of revolution. Here it is enough to note that beginning with a Utopian vision precludes the possibility of differentiating between situations where revolution is justified and others where it is not. The alternative to a Utopian vision is an understanding of the relativity of societies, acceptance of the fact that in man's present provisional state no social order is entirely satisfactory but we are committed to work, by revolution if necessary, to achieve a better order than that which now prevails. This approach may be less emotionally rousing than Utopianism, but it is a more solid base for serious revolution.

The determination of "real injury suffered" is evaded by the revolutionary *illuminati* who refuse to deal with specific injuries, who begin with the premise that a social order is corrupt, exploitative, and generally ripe for overthrow. From that premise, anything good about the social order in question is only a cleverly disguised evil designed to deflect radicals from their revolutionary purpose. There is a large truth in this analysis, explaining its hold upon contemporary radicalism.

The clever corruption of Western democracy, Marcuse says, is evident in its ability to avoid head-on collision with ideas and visions that call it into question. The most damning indictment is readily assimilated by the society's rulers. If sublimated and repressed, the indictment has revolutionary potential and is dangerous to the regime. Therefore, the regime tries to avoid overt repression and "desublimates" the indictment. The idea is that when Eldridge Cleaver makes the coveted cover of *Time*, his protest against the American Way will become part of the American Way. Indeed the society's tolerance, and even celebration, of its most vigorous critics proves its worth. In current radical circles desublimation is usually called co-optation; the results are about the same.

The strategy of desublimation is very real and very clever. Every would-be revolutionary must learn to resist its subtle wiles, or else be, as they say, co-opted. This is not the only peril to the revolutionary, however. Once the revolutionary sees how desublimation is used to control public opinion and nullify radical challenges, he himself may fall victim to his own insight. That is, he extends his insight into the strategy of desublimation by making it a working assumption in his total social analysis. This logical fallacy quickly leads to talking nonsense. His analysis becomes a matter of dogmatic commitment that is oblivious to the possibility of anything really happening in the society.

For instance, he sees a particular injustice, say the hunger of sharecroppers in Mississippi. Imagine that social critics raise an outcry about this situation, enlist the media in the cause, and as a consequence the hungry Mississippians are supplied with food on a secure basis. Such things do happen, not often enough or fast enough, but they happen. The fact is that a particular grievance was redressed. One might say that the particular injustice was only part of a much larger problem that touches on the whole economic and social structure of Mississippi, and he would be right in saying that. It is also possible that the redressing of this one grievance might distract attention from the larger problem. But it is nonsense to say that the particular grievance was not redressed. If one believes it is a good thing for hungry people to have food, it is nonsense to say that the redressing of this grievance was, in itself, a step backward rather than forward.

The counterargument to the above is that, in terms of forwarding the revolution, getting food for the hungry without changing the System is regressive. It tends to reinforce the impression that the System is working all right. Thus every reform, every change short of revolution, is counterrevolutionary. Then the question arises, why do we want revolution? Is it not to correct injustices that cannot be corrected without fundamental change in the political, economic and social system? If so, we must specify what these injustices are. And we must be clear about the limits of reform, even the most radical reform. It is not enough to say the system itself is unjust, for the System is not some mythological "thing." It is the conglomerate of interacting and interlocked systems of policies and habits by which power is exercised and human behavior is conditioned. The System is nothing less than the society itself.

Measured by the standard of an imagined Utopia, every "society itself" is unjust. Measured by the standards of history—and this is the only choice we have in a world far short of Utopia—some societies are more just than others. This judgment about relative justice is to be made on the basis of specific injustices and the way they are handled by a society. Such a basis for judgment is excluded if we fall victim to the subtle distortion of applying the desublimation insight as a general theory that controls our social anaylsis. In that case we make an a priori judgment that turns injustice into justice and makes of every reform a further injustice. Revolutionary thought then becomes a metaphysical game of enormous intricacy which only a limited number of the initiated can play.

If we are to determine "the real injury suffered" we must first decide what constitutes an injury. This, in turn, requires a clear notion of what values are so important to us that we are prepared to take up arms against their systematic violation. Some earlier Americans had their little lists of what constituted inviolable rights. "Life, liberty and the pursuit of happiness" is one such summary. Earlier versions substituted "property" for "liberty" and made it "public happiness" instead of the Declaration of Independence's "happiness" which has since been subject to restrictively privatized interpretations. Today we might be inclined to state the elementary values in less grandiose terms. We cannot adequately discuss the question of elementary values here, but I would suggest that a contemporary statement should have among its ingredients: adequate food, shelter, and medical care; freedom from physical terror; freedom of expression; a modicum of participation in those decisions that affect one's daily life.

This may not seem like a very adventuresome set of demands. Perhaps it isn't, but it is a great deal more than millions of Americans have, and it constitutes a fantastic dream for the majority of the world's population.

The values set forth above may seem to be the conventional values of "decadent, liberal, Western democracy." In a sense they are. But they are also the values shared by most human beings; if they are not universal, they come pretty close to universality. The reader can revise, refine and reshuffle the list to his own satisfaction. But one must begin with some statement of values before he can determine "the real injury suffered." Conservatives might argue that the last value—a modicum of participation in those decisions that affect one's daily life—is not really essential; that, if the other needs are satisfied, it is all right to leave the decision-making to others. The reader might argue this point, but if he does, he should know he is drawing on a tradition of Western democratic thought rather than on the tradition of French or Marxist revolutionary thought.

On the other side, the Marxist would argue that "freedom of expression" is a bourgeois value that has to be surrendered in order to further the revolution. In situations where real injury is suffered against the other values, I might agree with the Marxist, at least to the extent of a temporary suspension of freedom of expression. This decision, of course, involves us in all the problems mentioned earlier in connection with the accountability of revolutionary leadership to the sovereign people. These are the inescapable problems in making a revolution.

After the reader has drawn up his list of values, which to violate would mean "real injury suffered," the question of the justness of the revolution is not resolved. We have said that the question of justice is relative, but relative to what? If we take my little list of values and use it to compare the Soviet Union with the United States, we might decide that revolution would be exceedingly just in the Soviet Union but not in the United States. I believe a fair-minded person would grant that the United States comes off looking relatively good when compared to most other nations. But such comparisons miss the point.

Each of the values I have listed above is violated in the American social system. Millions are denied food, shelter, and medical care that are anywhere near adequate, even, in many cases, to maintain life itself. They are terrorized by police, criminals, and a court system indifferent to the poor. For all Americans, freedom of expression is severely limited by vested interests controlling the mass media. For a radical minority, repression is more overt. As for participating in the decisions which affect their daily lives, the unresponsiveness of the national political system has been illuminated by such events as the 1968 Democratic Convention at Chicago. Compared to most local and state governments, the national government is the epitome of democratic sensitivity. The point is not that the United States social system violates these values less than most other countries. The present situation must be compared with what *could be* the situation in the United States. And it must be measured against the price it exacts for its maintenance from the poor in other parts of the world.

It is fair and necessary to compare the present situation of a society against the possibilities that can reasonably be projected. The justice of a revolution in the United States depends upon our judgment as to whether the specific injuries mentioned can be corrected without revolution. This gets us into the question of revolution as a "last resort," a question we will take up later. The issue here is only to clarify the nature of the decision that must be made about "real injury suffered."

A second point of comparison in determining the "real injury suffered" is the influence of American power in the world. It may be that we consider conditions reasonably satisfactory for the people of the United States, but there is still the question as to whether these conditions are secured at the expense of other peoples. A revolutionary judgment must transcend the narrow limitations of nationalism. If we determine that there is not real and irreformable injury suffered by the people of the United States, but that American power in other parts of the world (Latin America, for instance) does do such injury, we have laid part of the basis for a just revolution at the center of that power, namely in the United States itself. Note we have used the terms "real *and irreformable.*" We will return to the condition of irreformability.

Before leaving the question of injury, we should note that "real injury suffered" is present only where the injury is systematic rather than occasional or accidental. As in our previous discussion of legitimate authority, it is necessary to be able to specify the responsible parties and policies. If the injury is attributable to ordinary human mistakes or to physical circumstances, then it is something other than that injury that warrants revolution. One economist has remarked that the economic situation of a certain Latin American country is like three men selling two oranges to one another. Objective conditions such as the absence of capital and parched, unproductive land are not amenable to political exhortations or revolutions. This is one of the hard lessons that the new regime in Cuba had to learn. While it may be useful for propaganda purposes to blame every inconvenience and misfortune on the ruling elite, honesty in determining the justice of revolution requires a careful distinction between rhetoric and fact. In New York City the supporters of Mario Procaccino attributed to Mayor Lindsay's influence such developments as women not wearing bras and the "insolence" of young blacks. It may have been good politics, but it is doubtful that Lindsay should get credit for these happy trends. Neither should regimes be blamed for every trouble that afflicts a society.

In summary, "in response to real injury suffered" means that the regime has in its practice declared war on the people. That there is a systematic violation of elementary and clearly specified rights.

We have asked what it means for a revolution to be declared by legitimate authority and in response to real injury suffered. The third hurdle to be cleared by a just revolution is that it be "undertaken only after all reasonable means of peaceful settlement have been exhausted."

At the End of Our Tether

A man makes revolution because he has no other choice. A boy makes revolution because he has no other thought. If revolution is the goal, nothing other than revolution will do. If a changed society is the goal, there may be several ways of getting at it. I have a middle-aged and rather influential friend who claims to be a veteran of the International Brigade of the Spanish Civil War (I do not doubt it) and is determined that this time around we will not miss the opportunity for revolution. For him every black man who makes it into the construction unions is a setback, each step toward a guaranteed annual income is a disaster, and the prospect of the war in Vietnam ending is one of unmitigated gloom. America needs a revolution, he believes, in order to give the black man an equal break in employment, to secure the economic rights overlooked by the Constitution, and to bring an end to imperialist wars. If these things are already happening, he fears he may yet be cheated of his chance to die on the barricades. My friend is prematurely worried. He exaggerates the progress being made in resolving this society's problems. For the foreseeable future, revolution will present itself as a lively option for many devoted to radical change. What is unhappy about my friend is that he really wants revolution, in a very real sense he needs revolution. He needs revolution the way the American Legionnaires need war. They hang about their halls of drunken reminiscence recalling exaggerated deeds of glory and bemoaning the pinkos in high places who deny them the satisfaction of a no-holds-barred brawl with the Commies. It is sick. It is sick, whether the blood lust is in the name of patriotism or of revolution, whether invoked for the "free world" or for the wretched of the earth.

Violence is the elixir of the weak. In the alchemy of conflict men imagine that the base metal of their lives is transformed into heroic gold. Go to the hangouts of the Veterans of Foreign Wars or to the dens of the American Minutemen or down the dormitory hall to the room where freshman radicals, who discovered Fanon last week, rap about revolution. The legitimations for violence are dramatically different, but the celebration of the virtues of violence is the same. Violence cuts through life's ambiguities, proves manhood, and separates the damned from the elect. The reasons for revolution need not be given in advance, we are told. It is only in the revolutionary struggle itself that man and his possibilities are revealed, the new order will emerge from blood and ashes. It is a faith worthy of a mystic. The most bizarre versions of the transubstantiation of the body and blood of Jesus in the Mass cannot equal the cultic language of revolution in gory impact. The revolutionary convert is born again into the mystical body of Che Guevara, the *communio sanctorum* of the committed. Have we not seen the photographs of the corpse taken down from the cross? This time, surrounded not by Sadducees but by functionaries of the Bolivian junta, done in not by Roman legions but by the occupying forces of the CIA. Incarnate once more, not as the wandering rabbi from Galilee but as the guerrilla fighter heralding a new order. Yes, Che too is risen and present in the fervor of the apostolic band that bears the blood-stained banner in His Name on the barricades of revolution. It is a religion; violence and the talk of violence is its sacrament. The suspension of intelligence is the only fee required for initiation into the fellowship of the revolutionary elect.

Those of us who already have a religion and those who

wish to reject religion must take a different approach to revolution. Revolution is not the goal but the means, the means of last resort. Certainly there are situations in our world where sober men are forced to revolution. Persuasion, negotiation, litigation, confrontation—all means of peaceful settlement are exhausted. Those who are radically devoted to social justice must take inventory of their resources in their situation. They must have the "purity of heart" to disdain dramatic posturing so that when driven to take life it is truly an act affirming respect for life, not a willingness to sacrifice others to indulge their need for excitement or an effort to prove by blood the seriousness of their commitment.

Taking inventory of our resources in the United States requires that we not confuse our impetuosity with our political analysis. Recently I saw a young man join, with great trepidation, his first picket line. The issue had to do with community control of New York City schools. In the course of the day several people were arrested, and afterward there was a meeting of the insurgents to evaluate the day's events. Our young man, making up in eloquence what he lacked in experience, proclaimed that we had marched and been beaten and abused and arrested long enough. "If all they [the rulers of the school system] can understand is violence, then I say let's give them violence!" His debut in the role of Patrick Henry was met with laughter by some and with indignation by others. Laughter because most of us do our share of posturing and can be sympathetic to the fault in others. Indignation because such posturing can divert strategy for radical change, in this case control of public facilities by the poor, who are after all, in their communities, the public.

The confusion of impetuosity with political analysis not only prevents us from determining what constitutes the justice of a revolution, but also threatens the success of revolution. In building a revolutionary movement one does not act like a street-corner evangelist, asking people right off to join up for the revolution. "Brother, do you want to be saved?" is a good opener if one's purpose is to enlist the neurotically dependent and fugitives from other gods that failed. In building a revolutionary movement the immediate appeal is to work together for a better society marked by those things that men of good will desire for themselves and their brothers. There is indeed a movement, from outrage with things as they are and hope for something better, through reformist efforts to the conclusion that change can come only through revolution. It is a disservice to the revolution to try to short-circuit the process by which revolutionary conviction, as distinct from sentiment, is created.

Michael Harrington of *The Other America* fame is fond of saying that successful reform can have revolutionary consequences while unsuccessful revolution leads only to frustration and destruction. It is equally true that unsuccessful reform can lead to revolution, and that the chances of success for the revolution are increased in proportion to the degree it is true that "all reasonable means of peaceful settlement have been exhausted." Thus, again, it appears that considerations of justice and considerations of strategy complement one another.

Those who have arrived at the decision for revolution have come by different routes. Some have come out of the great tribulation of years of earnest struggle for reform. Others have arrived by way of more theoretical considerations in which it has became obvious that the goals they seek cannot be achieved within the framework of the prevailing order. If they are Americans, they have concluded that their search for social justice compels them to join with others in working for the forceful overthrow of this political and economic system and the Constitution of the United States of America that sustains it.

A person has not arrived at the decision for revolution simply because he is prepared to work outside the context of the Constitution and its laws. A decision for civil disobedience, whether peaceful and non-violent or riotous and violent, is not a decision for revolution. On the contrary, such disruptions of the society's habits are usually aimed not at the overthrow of the system but at provoking and pressuring the system to work more effectively. This is reformism, although, to be sure, radical reformism. The decision for revolution is made at the point where it becomes inescapably clear that no amount of political activism, protest or pressure—legal or extra-legal—can make this constitutional order work to the benefit of American citizens and millions of others who are under the sway of American power. I believe few Americans have made this decision. Before making it, we might take a candid look at our inventory of alternatives to revolution.

Critics of the Movement say its adherents can see nothing good in America. This is patent nonsense. It is impossible that a country of two hundred million people has not in two hundred years produced much that is noble, beautiful and worthy of man's dignity. During much of that time, and in spite of slavery, lynchings, and massacres, honorable men could view the American experiment as reason to hope for the world's liberation. As Staughton Lynd points out in *Intellectual Origins of American Radicalism,* much of the revolutionary consciousness of the present is an effort to revive the best of the American experiment, to call America back to her nobler self. The decision for revolution today is a shoddy and deceitful decision if it is based on the lie that the American tradition is unmitigated iniquity, that there have been no humanizing moments, no progress in uplifting the downtrodden. Some radical rhetoric has it that the black man today is as oppressed as he was under slavery in the South. There may be some sophisticated, perhaps esoteric, interpretation by which that statement can be made less the fatuity than, on the face of it, it surely is.

It is no compromise of one's incisive analysis to acknowledge that, by any human index, the black American has it better now than he did when he was bartered as chattel with absolutely no rights legal or personal. Anyone who contests this should be asked in all seriousness whether he is ready to support a return to the system of slavery. A long list could be drawn up of similarly elemental improvements that have occurred within the framework of the U. S. Constitution. But to conclude from such a list that the United States is not in need of revolution is the conservative's grave misunderstanding of the debate raging today.

The long list of improvements is challenged by three basic observations. First, in all the areas to which one might point to illustrate improvement, the change has been tortuously slow and is discouragingly incomplete. This is true of black-white relations in particular, of minority group rights in general, and of the quality of life secured by the majority of Americans who have supposedly made it. On the last score, it might be argued that human failure is in direct ratio to economic success in a consumer society. Second, there are new and unprecedented (at least in the American experience) evils today, evils that can be attributed to American successes, thus making ours a "society against itself." Among these is our reaching the crisis point in technological pollution leading to ecological disaster, the canceling out of the future by nuclear weaponry, the persistent rotting of our cities, and the bondage of the world's poor in the cooperative grip of the greed of the rich nations, led by the United States. No long list of improvements can assuage the impact of these evils. Third and most ominous, the challenge is raised whether America's political-legal-economic machinery has the strength remaining to turn the tide of evil. The first two challenges, insofar as they touch on the justice of revolution, overlap with the previous section on "real injury suffered." It is the third challenge that directly concerns us here.

To decide whether the resources for change have been exhausted requires an examination of those activities and institutions from which we expect the thrust for change to emerge, or by which needed change is implemented. The public school system, for example, claims to inculcate the ideas of America's revolutionary tradition. Yet increasingly the teaching and administrative bureaucracies of American elementary education have isolated themselves in specialization, coming out of their educational enclave only when teachers find it necessary to fight against the people for their job conditions and their right to exercise complete control over their slice of the system.

"It is secrecy, mystery, that is everywhere the soul of bureaucracy," wrote Marx in his youth, and in few places is this as true as in the American public school system which was devised to pass on the flame of the democratic dream. As Ivan Illich, a contemporary prophet, says, "The American public school system has acquired a power to intimidate similar to that possessed by the church in the middle ages. 'Going to school' is a cultic activity mandated not by common sense but by superstition."

The private church-related elementary schools have, far from providing creative diversity, largely imitated the public system and, too often, served as a refuge for parents who refuse to have their children attend racially integrated classes. The development of a genuinely pluralistic system of schools—run by community and special interest groups, teaching values that offend some Americans —seems a long way off. In short, it does not appear probable that the elementary educational system is likely to produce a generation fired by a radical determination for change.

The high schools are, for the most part, extensions of the coercion to conform that is practiced in elementary schools. In the last year or two there has been a growing insurgency among high school students, but the same ambiguities surround this as surround insurgency on the university campus. So much has been written about campus radicalism that we will not dwell on it here, except to ask whether the protest against the university being treated as a factory in the "knowledge industry" is not being replaced by an equally unproductive notion of the university as the home of the youth culture.* Does student control of the university advance social change outside the university which is, after all, something of a protected enclave? Is the university really to be the organizing center and staging area for revolutionary change, or is the danger, as Herbert Marcuse has warned, that the university may be destroyed and with it the institutional base for the change that is envisioned? These are among the questions to be answered by prospective revolutionaries before concluding that "all reasonable means of peaceful settlement have been exhausted."

American religion is, according to some analysts, an institution of hope. The church has come a long way from being, or at least being exclusively, the consoler of the Babbitts who seek divine approval for their abuse of the powerless. In the last decade of American life, especially on issues of race and war, some of the most penetrating critiques and proposals have come from American religion, as well as vigorous radical leadership in the form of the Berrigans, Groppis, Coffins, and a host of "new breed" clergy. Religion is still the largest voluntary enterprise in America, with more than 44 per cent of the population attending services on the average weekend. But that figure is declining, and the reason, at least in part, is that the clergy seem to their congregations to be too far out on social questions. Malcolm Muggeridge, a cantankerous but worthy critic of "relevant religion," predicts that shortly institutional religion will be like NATO, a headquarters without any armies. I have some ideas on how religion might drive toward a more productive future, but that is the subject of another essay. The issue here is whether, as unlikely as it may seem to some,

---

* This is Peter Berger's question and I leave it to him to develop it further. I agree with his essential analysis but, as should be obvious, draw from it somewhat different conclusions.

American religion is a resource for radical change that has not yet been exhausted.

A funny thing that happened on the way to the revolution is the system of electoral politics. Eastland, Daley, Chicago '68, Richard Nixon, Safeguard, Spiro Agnew—to name it is to indict it. If the names were different— Kennedy, McCarthy, McGovern, Cleaver, Stokes, Seales, and Lindsay, for instances—would it *really* make any difference? Yes, we all know the orthodox answer, that it wouldn't make any difference because it is the System, not the faces, that must be changed. But be fair and imagine that the encrusted seniority rule of Congress were shattered and the White House occupied by the person of your choice. Take into account the kinds of decisions that would be made, remembering the Constitution's proven flexibility in accommodating executive and congressional programs of social improvement. Would it make any difference? I quite literally challenge the sanity of anyone who answers no. Of course, the chances of all this happening seem somewhat remote and I will understand if the reader, impatient with these academic questions, picks up and continues on his way to the revolution.

Admittedly, the System itself must be changed. What is the future of minorities, for instance, in a system committed to majority rule? The issue touches not only on racial minorities but also on the minority of the poor and, tying together three exploited factors, on the urban black poor. What are the alternatives to oppressive majority rule? One looks in vain for other social systems where the rights of minorities are better protected. But, as we have seen, other societies are not the relevant point of comparison, just as our Utopian hopes are not. The United States has, it is commonly argued, a corrective resource to prevent, or at least limit, the tyranny of the majority. On his way to the revolution, one should consider the court system.

The courtroom is allegedly the free forum in which, defying the orthodoxies of popular opinion and the compromises of electoral politics, fundamental challenges can be raised to the system. There are times when the courts do seem to acquit themselves in line with this claim. It is probable, for instance, that the 1954 school desegregation decision of the Supreme Court would not have been made the law of the land had it been left to the Congress or to a poll of popular sentiment. Such decisions seem relatively rare, however, and, as in the case of school desegregation, extremely weak when it comes to implementation.

The courts dare not penetrate to the heart of the power elite's decisions by overruling, for example, the priority of death over life in the nation's budget, declaring it violates the Constitution's declared purpose to "promote the general Welfare, and secure the Blessings of Liberty to ourselves and our Posterity." Even if the courts should exercise such authority, would it not seem a dangerously arbitrary thing that so few men could wield so much power? The danger will probably become clearer now that the "Warren Court" is a thing of the past. We may be glad enough if the court system and the Supreme Court limit themselves largely to questions of personal rights, rather than restructuring the System in accord with the professed social purposes of the Constitution. Indeed we will be more than glad, even delighted, if the courts continue to provide the modicum of protection for civil liberties by which fundamental challenges can be raised in other forums.

Nowhere has the legal system seemed, in the eyes of contemporary radicals, to be more impotent than in its inability to challenge the Vietnam war and the military apparatus that supports and, quite likely, requires, war. Several trials—e.g. Spock-Coffin, Catonsville 9, Milwaukee 14—demonstrate the difficulties of democratic debate within the legal context. In each instance, the defense attempted to put the government on trial, contesting the legality and morality of the Vietnam war and of conscription. In each instance the judge ruled such a challenge out of order, instructing the jury that its only business was to determine whether the defendants were guilty of the specific offense charged.

The questions surrounding Vietnam as an undeclared war and the draft as a form of involuntary servitude are well known. Given the timidity of the lords of the American judiciary, it appears that these questions will never be aired in open court. Only the most innocent of citizens can fail to perceive the servility of the courts, which is a result of their dependence on political and popular pressures. The conviction of Huey Newton and several hundred citizens who in Chicago '68 dared to exercise their supposed right to free expression stands in eloquent witness against those who would make the case for the integrity and vitality of American law.

In 1735 Andrew Hamilton addressed himself to a colonial jury in New York in defense of John Peter Zenger. Zenger was accused of publishing seditious tracts. There was no doubt that he had indeed done so. Hamilton insisted, however, that the twelve men of the jury were in duty bound "to see with their own eyes, to hear with their own ears, and to make use of their consciences and understandings in judging of the lives, liberties, or estates of their fellow subjects." That is, the jury had the duty not only of determining the *fact,* whether or not Zenger had done what he was accused of doing, but also the *law,* whether or not the law by which he was accused was valid. The jury acquitted Zenger. Ironically, in the defense of the Catonsville 9, chief counsel William Kunstler was citing the exact words of Hamilton when he was interrupted by the judge who ruled any judgment of *law* out of order. The same ruling has been made time and again in trials of resisters and of others who have engaged in various forms of civil disobedience. As one juror remarked after the Spock-Coffin trial in Boston, "We found them guilty as accused by the judge." The judge had so narrowly restricted the issue to be tried that the realities of war and domestic coercion, without which the trial made no sense and in fact would not have occurred, were deemed totally irrelevant.

The meaning of all this for our discussion of revolution is made clear by Professor Joseph L. Sax of the University of Michigan Law School writing in the *Yale Review:*

> Those who think resisters are tearing at the fabric of the society might wish to consider the possibility that a society is best able to survive if it permits a means for taking an issue back to the public over the heads of public officialdom: when it recognizes that a government may have so implicated itself in a wretched policy that it needs to be extricated by popular repudiation in a forum more immediately available—and less politically compromised—than a ballot box.

The notion that a jury is trier of the law as well as of the fact is moribund, but not dead.

No doubt a stronger case can be made for the legal system as an agent of radical change than is suggested here. But so long as the courts are plagued by their present timidities and inequities they will, in the minds of most radicals, have little power to undermine the belief that "all reasonable means of peaceful settlement have been exhausted."

Of the agencies that purport to offer leverage for change, education, religion, electoral politics, and the law have been tried and found wanting. No agency is of course entirely satisfactory; and of course there are signs of hope for those determined to find such signs, and of course there is no end to new variations on old tactics that can be tried within these institutions. But there is an end to patience. Increasingly social zealots have moved outside these institutions into demonstration, dramatic protest, riotous insurrection and calculated terrorism. And increasingly such actions have invoked the specter and reality of repression. The growing gap between radicalism and the blue-collar worker, and even the majority of the really poor, is interpreted in different and conflicting

ways. For those who want reform, the gap is disastrous.
For those set upon Revolution Now, backlash and repression are welcomed as prelude to the moment of truth
in which the decadence of the System will be exposed, the
superstructure of the American Way will collapse, and
the new man in the new order will emerge Phoenix-like
from the ashes. Polarization is prelude to the revolution.

Still others recognize that America is not yet in a pre-
revolutionary situation. It is too early, they say, to know
whether all the means of settlement have been exhausted.
The task now is to build a movement, reaching out to
the great newly washed of blue-collar workers, aimed
at radical change. Relentless efforts for radical change
on all fronts will alone reveal what powers of adapta-
bility yet remain in the old institutions. In a sense,
revolutionaries do not decide for revolution but, as discussed in the previous section, the regime declares war,
inviting the response of revolution.

Finally, there are those who are not waiting. They
may be building a movement, but it is quite clearly
in their minds a revolutionary movement, and is only
a question of time before the revolutionary intent becomes
explicit. Meanwhile they can work with others in the
intermediate phase of pressing for radical reform. But
for themselves the question is settled, they are in the
business of making revolution.

The "last resort" clause does not require the responsible
revolutionary to try personally every means of achieving
change, for, as we have observed, strategies for change
are endless in their variety. "Trying new ways to reform
this society is like trying to make better love to an old
whore by following a manual that outlines a hundred
positions for intercourse. She's still an old whore." Thus
one rebel describes the dilemma. But one way of determining that the society is an old whore is precisely by demon-
strating that it does not have the capacity for radical
change. The argument is excruciatingly circular: reform is
out because the society is irreformable, but only efforts

at reform reveal the irreformability of the society. The a priori assumption that revolution is the only way is both unpersuasive in recruiting for the revolutionary movement and, for the revolutionary leader, a commitment built on sand; in the storm of struggle it will shift and erode, resulting in the collapse of the movement's plausibility.

Reaching the end of our tether and deciding for revolution should be the result not of hot-blooded passion but of cool analysis within the context of historical perspective and a candid assessment of the possibilities of the future. Come the revolution, there will be time and need for passion. Now we must put in order the priorities of our goals and seek some other way of their fulfillment. If we find there is no other way, it may be that revolution is the way. At least the revolution that emerges from this earnest search will have met one criterion of justice, namely that it will be undertaken after all reasonable means of peaceful settlement have been exhausted.

A just revolution is declared by legitimate authority in response to real injury as a last resort, and is prosecuted with good intention. Our attention now turns to the meaning of "good intention" in making revolution.

Intention and Purity of Heart

"Purity of heart," wrote Søren Kierkegaard, "is to will one thing." Kierkegaard cites the example of Abraham in his willingness to kill his son Isaac, and thereby abandon hope for the promise given to his future generations, in obedience to God's command. Other examples are Socrates' taking his own life in devotion to the State, Jesus going to the cross in total commitment to the gospel of the coming Kingdom of God, Martin Luther King surrendering to his dream that the black man will redeem the

American experiment. Not all revolutionaries will be saints and heroes, but the revolution itself depends upon the transparency and intensity of revolutionary allegiance.

The mendicant monk of a revolutionary church, Mikhail Bakunin (1814–76), wrote with his disciple S. G. Nechaev *Catechism of a Revolutionist,* which set forth the singleness of heart that is demanded:

> The Revolutionist is a doomed man. He has no private interests, no affairs, sentiments, ties, property nor even a name of his own. His entire being is devoured by one purpose, one thought, one passion—the revolution . . . Heart and soul, not merely by word but by deed, he has severed every link with the social order and with the entire civilized world; with the laws, good manners, conventions, and morality of that world. He is its merciless enemy and continues to inhabit it with only one purpose— to destroy it . . . He despises public opinion. He hates and despises the social morality of his time, its motives and manifestations. Everything which promotes the success of the revolution is moral, everything which hinders it is immoral . . . The nature of the true revolutionist excludes all romanticism, all tenderness, all ecstasy, all love.

After more than twenty efforts to organize revolts, Bakunin lost his faith in "spontaneous popular insurrection" as the method of overthrowing regimes. He died a disillusioned man in Berne, Switzerland, but his example and writings remained a major influence on revolutionaries, including Lenin. And *Catechism of a Revolutionist* has proved itself a classic in revolutionary literature. It is, I believe, a brutal and dehumanizing prescription for fanaticism but, nevertheless, a powerful statement of the dynamics of revolutionary singleness of heart.

A just revolution, our fourth criterion suggests, is one in which those engaged have good intention. Good intention is not the same thing as intensity, for one could in his magnificent fervor be magnificently wrong. Here again the reader must develop for himself some idea of which intentions are worthy and which should be repudiated. My idea of the latter is close to the thinking of other ethicists who have worked with the "just war" approach. Vengeance, for instance, may be understandable, but as an intention in waging revolution is unworthy. There are other intentions to be repudiated: the private search for fulfillment, resolving identity problems through conflict, the whole militarist heritage of "gore and glory"; the lust for power itself; sadism and related psychoses; perfectionism, the belief that an unambiguously good social order can be established; the intention to destroy rather than transform the society. The list could be expanded and is in all cases closely correlated with what one posits as the goals of revolution. In the section on "real injury suffered" I spelled out what some of those humanizing and democratizing goals are. Good intention, then, is quite simply the pursuit of those goals.

"Good intention" is not, as it is in the *Catechism of a Revolutionist,* devotion to the revolution itself. That is, the "will to revolution" is not self-legitimating. This insight underlies the whole discussion of just revolution. Were the will to revolution self-legitimating, there could be no just revolution because there could be no unjust revolution. The very term "just revolution" assumes the possibility of an unjust revolution.

Good intention is more a matter of revolutionary objective than it is of purity of heart. It is more a political than a psychological reality. The intention, the deed, and the motivation are interdependent. If they are in too obvious conflict with one another, the revolution suffers a plausibility collapse. What happens here is not very different from what happens with governments in general. When a South American junta claims to represent the peasantry's desire for freedom, and at the same time protects by force the inequity of two per cent of the people owning eighty per cent of the land, the credibility of the junta is called into question. Similarly, America's economic aid to South Africa and military support of

206 *Richard John Neuhaus*

Franco Spain are deeds in glaring contradiction to its professed intention of defending the "free" world. Or, in the area of personal motivation, Lyndon Johnson's obscene use of Albert Schweitzer's phrase "reverence for life" in his televised appeal to blacks to cool it following the assassination of Dr. King illustrates the kind of contradiction that quickly discredits leadership. In these instances governments survive because they can rely on instruments of coercion that are not available to the revolution.

A revolutionary movement is more dependent on a concordance between declared intention, deed, and private motivation. In the revolution, purity of heart is inextricably related to good intention because, as we have seen, the leadership and morale call for charismatic support to a degree not required by ruling regimes. Toward the end of his life Malcolm X "realized how very dangerous it is for people to hold any human being in [too high] esteem, especially to consider anyone some sort of 'divinely guided' and 'protected' person." The drift toward idolization must be constantly resisted, and nowhere is the drift stronger than in the demands it makes for purity of heart. The revolutionary movement, it is insisted, must be untainted by the corruptions of the decadent enemy regime.

The French Revolution floundered and failed in large part because its leaders demanded a degree of purity of heart so extreme that even the most noble intentions could not live up to the demand. This preoccupation with the heart led to a "Law of Suspects" that caught everyone involved in a net of suspicion. Hannah Arendt writes, "Robespierre's insane lack of trust in others, even in his closest friends, sprang ultimately from his not so insane but quite normal suspicion of himself. Since his very credo forced him to play the 'incorruptible' in public every day and to display his virtue, to open his heart as he understood it, at least once a week, how could he be sure that he was not the one thing he probably feared most in his life, a hypocrite?" Today we see the same disastrous process at work in many radical circles. There are vague accusations and counteraccusations about who has "sold out," betraying "the spirit of the revolution" and the such.

Good intention, then, must be defined in terms of program, of political goal. Surely revolution involves the heart but, in the infinite variety of human emotions, the heart cannot be the point of reference in determining the revolution's intention. This becomes clear when we stop thinking of the revolution as a politicized Woodstock Festival where people celebrate their unity in a new liberation of the senses and where answers blow in the wind.

The revolution is not a happening but a program; an adventurous, exhilarating program, perhaps, but a program nonetheless. And the revolution's intention is assured not by sincerity and intensity alone but by the evolvement of a lucid agenda that can enlist people of disparate cultural backgrounds and temperaments. Unless the good intention is credibly and clearly articulated, the revolution becomes no revolution at all, but merely clusterings within the youth culture of radical debating clubs devoted to mutual support, therapy, and endless cross-examinations about purity of heart.

Some aspects of the revolution's intention, it is true, cannot be spelled out in advance, only in a synthesis of action and reflection is the direction clarified. The Movement today is highly critical of the non-ideological, problem-solving pragmatists who dominate the several American establishments. Yet many revolutionaries in the Movement seem equally hostile to ideology, substituting emotion and sensuality for pragmatism. This tendency, which precludes any clear development of intention, must be seen as a fundamentally counterrevolutionary force. "Action! Deeds! These alone matter. Leave the theory to the scribblers!" was the motto of Mussolini. The political possibilities of turning on and blowing the mind were not lost on the Fascists. Mussolini remarked, "Democracy has deprived the life of the people of 'style': that is, a line of conduct, the color, the strength, the picturesque, the unexpected, the mystical; in sum, all that counts in the soul of the masses. We play the lyre on all its strings: from violence to religion, from art to politics."

The intention of the revolution should not be so doctrinally defined that it allows for no flexibility, no growth in the light of experience and action. Nor should the insistence on pure intention be so severe that it leads to a deceptive self-righteousness that can only end in suspicion and disillusionment. Any movement of broad appeal will have within it all the ambiguities that mark the human condition itself. There will be the passions of power lust and vengeance. Unavoidably, some people will seek in revolutionary action the satisfactions others find by climbing the ladder of the corporate hierarchy and yet others in careers in the military. Unavoidably, some people will be motivated by a desire to "get Whitey," while others will be eager to settle old scores with persons and institutions of their chosen hatred.

Personally, one can aim for purity of heart, but the most that can be hoped for the revolutionary movement is that it will have integrity. This means an integral relationship, a wholeness, of stated purpose, action, and heart. This is the combination that sustains physically and emotionally the enormous discipline required for revolution. In the belief that he was struggling within this context of integrity, Che Guevara could write about "a will power that I have polished with the relish of an artist and it will sustain a pair of flaccid legs and tired lungs. I will do it." Such is the context of integrity needed to sustain a revolution declared by legitimate authority, in response to real injury, undertaken as a last resort, and engaged in with good intention. Without such integrity, no serious person would pay the high price of revolution. Which brings us to the fifth criterion of justice.

The High Price of Revolution

The "just war" approach to conflict is not acclaimed by everyone. There are those who believe, for instance, that its provisions about "legitimate authority" are tied to an outmoded notion of national sovereignty, and that its ideas about "moral means" assume understandings among gentlemen knights that are absurd in an age of nuclear terror. Although the just-war approach is embattled on many scores, even its most severe critics admit the continuing relevance of some of its insights. Almost everyone agrees with this fifth measure, that a just war is one in which the damage likely to be incurred by the war must not be disproportionate to the injury suffered. *Almost* everyone, since some devotees of the "better dead than red" school are still with us. The radical counterpart to John Birch fanaticism is the revolutionary who urges insurrection and "to hell with the consequences." The one believes there is no evil, not even death itself, greater than the evil of being dominated by "the Reds." The other believes nothing could be worse than the present capitalist-imperialist enslavement, therefore nothing is to be lost by revolution.

Just as we do not live in the best of all possible worlds, neither do we live in the worst. If 1200 black children in the South die from malnutrition each year, it could be 12,000. Vietnam could have been totally devastated by the use of nuclear weapons. The 850 Americans who are now in jails for resisting the war and the draft could be 8500, and so forth. This is not written in praise of things as they are. I recently attended a meeting where a consultant to the Pentagon seriously contended that people are inordinately upset by the damage in Vietnam. "You have to weigh what has been done," he said, "against what we have the power to do." This is madness, of course, for the proper measurement of what we do is against what we should do, not against what we could do. Following the Pentagon's logic, every murderer would be acquitted on the grounds that he could have murdered two people, or, if he did murder two, he could have made it three. It is a line of unreason worthy of *Alice's Adventures in Wonderland.*

It is nevertheless true that almost any situation could be worse than it is. Auschwitz and Dachau are probable exceptions, but those who assert that the American situation is a magnified Auschwitz are permitting their rhetoric to control their analysis. The same is true of most, if not all, other countries in which revolution is planned. The point is that revolution is a calculated risk that through the revolutionary struggle a bad situation will be made better rather than worse. One weighs the probable damage caused by the revolution against the real injury that provokes the revolution. If the probable damage is greater than the real injury, the revolution is unjust.

This fifth measurement, like the others, can be used by counterrevolutionary forces to inhibit and finally frustrate any act of insurrection. After all, the future is unknown to us, and if we wait until its imponderables are clarified there will never be a revolution. The standard ploy of the establishment is illustrated by one university administrator who reportedly challenged students who had taken over the administration building. "Here are the eight volumes detailing the university's budget," he said. "You may be right that the university is making mistakes in the allocation of its resources. So you people work through this material and show us where the budget should be corrected. Then your readiness to take over the school will be credible." Since the students had neither the time nor competence to understand the minutiae of the budget, and since the administration was not about to surrender its power simply because the students had mastered the details of operating the institution, the students rightly rejected this proposal as an insultingly obvious diversionary tactic.

Certain specifiable evils were being protested. The students' job was to pressure for change, the administration's was to implement the change. Such implementation may be difficult, but that, the students observe, is what the administrators are paid for. Similarly, those who call for a complete withdrawal from Vietnam are not responsible for working out the logistics of quartermastering. As William Sloane Coffin told Henry Kissinger, foreign policy adviser to Mr. Nixon, "Our job is to call for justice to roll down like mighty streams of water. Yours is to work out the irrigation system."

Revolution, however, is more than intensified protest. The protester highlights the evil and leaves the correction to others. This is a perfectly honorable role. Amos and Isaiah had no ambitions to become king; if they did, they would have lost their prophetic credentials. The revolution does aspire to replace the regime. It must therefore take more than a passing interest in irrigation systems. This does not mean that every contingency must be anticipated in advance. Total anticipation is impossible, at least if one accepts the metaphysics subscribed to by both Marxists and Christians in their understanding of history. In this view, the future is not captive to the past and present but is genuinely new. Therefore it is impossible to project from experience to date an exhaustive blueprint of the future. Nevertheless, some anticipation is possible; it is possible and necessary to establish the *probabilities* that attend a suggested course of action.

In his early and impressive *Reason and Revolution*, Herbert Marcuse seconds Hegel's assertion that Reason is man's most vital point of contact with the future's fulfillment. This Reason is, of course, dramatically different from the kind of "rationality" that emerged from nineteenth-century positivism and has led to the constricting pragmatism of our present decision-makers. Reason is the lively dynamic reaching out for possibilities as yet unrealized, entrusting itself to the promise of history's future. While there is a strong element of discontinuity, past experience is nevertheless in identifiable continuity with future experience; history is One.

This brief philosophical excursus is necessary because it touches on several factors present in contemporary thought about revolution. Because history is One, we should not be careless with the past. From past and present we receive "signals" of what is to be. There are, to use the term of theologian-philosopher Wolfhart Pannenberg, "proleptic events" which anticipate the future. The classic Marxist view, unlike the Christian notion of the coming of the Kingdom, holds to a rather brief period of history in which, through fundamental economic and political actions, the new order will be established. The reader must make up his mind about the implications of the failure of the revolution in the Soviet Union, China, and Cuba to confirm the Marxist expectation. Whatever else may be the virtues of these revolutions, they have not produced the freedom of the new man in the Stateless society. He may argue that each of these is a perversion of the revolution, but then he must contend with apologists for the American social experiment who likewise attribute present problems to a perversion of the American Dream and argue for a revival of the "real" intention of the Founding Fathers. Or the reader may say that the revolutions in Cuba, China, and the Soviet Union have not yet had time to work through the process leading to genuine socialism. Then, too, he has an argument on his hands with people like Walt Rostow who claim that American power in the Third World will produce humanization and development if we only give it time. In short, the arguments used to evade a statement regarding the shape of the future cut both ways.

Every statement about the future assumes ideology, an understanding about the nature of history and man. The Movement is rightly critical of those who rule the United States because they claim to be non-ideological pragmatists when, in fact, they simply refuse to put their ideology on the table where it can be examined and challenged. Our criticism also requires us, however, to come clean on our ideological presuppositions. This above all needs to be driven home: those would-be revolutionaries who think insurrection is a happening, who despise all efforts to anticipate the future, who disdain the role of Reason in revolutionary thought have abandoned both Marxist and Christian revolutionary traditions. What then are their presuppositions? If they say they don't want to be boxed-in ideologically, that they will handle problems as they arise, I am not persuaded. Dean Rusk and Richard Nixon make precisely the same excuse for their intellectual bankruptcy.

Considering a very limited slice of the future, what would be the probable damage inflicted by armed revolution in the United States? We will take up later the means used to wage such an effort: strategic bombings in urban facilities, calculated terrorism, torture, and the like. The means used will naturally have a bearing on the damage inflicted. Armed revolution, by its very definition, involves extensive resort to violence. The discussion of damage rules out the highly unlikely prospect that the regime will simply crumble of its own internal fear and decay. In any case, if it did collapse, it would probably collapse into the waiting arms of Rightist forces distinctly unsympathetic to the revolution.

Earnest revolutionaries must begin to make the kind of distasteful judgments now left to the Pentagon. What, for instance, is an "acceptable" number of casualties in a revolutionary struggle? Deaths, blindings, cripplings, children orphaned, and families homeless—this is the stuff of revolutionary strategy. In some countries where brutal despotism rides high, it is possible to make comparative

214 Richard John Neuhaus

calculations. The revolutionary can almost tabulate the starvations, imprisonments, executions, and other deprivations imposed by the regime and can, with reasonable confidence, draw comparisons with the projected cost of the revolution. It need not be a one-to-one comparison. If, for instance, there are a hundred executions per year under the regime, it may be that during the years of revolutionary struggle that number would rise to five hundred or more (executed by both sides), but *in the long run* the success of the revolution would mean fewer people being killed and a better life for all.

In the United States of the foreseeable future, armed revolution will inevitably raise the level of suffering and death over what it is now. On the other hand, if one includes in his calculation the suffering American power exacts in the Third World, he may come to a conclusion more favorable to revolution. In making such a calculation, however, he should, as was discussed in connection with "real injury suffered," be reasonably certain that it is in fact American power that exacts such suffering from the world's poor and also that a revolution in the United States would substantively alleviate that suffering. Such revolutionary projections demand great self-restraint in setting aside generalized radical slogans and calculating the future in comformity with the Reason that impels us to freedom.

So we compare the high price of revolution with the high price of not having a revolution. This brief section has simply pointed up a few of the factors to be entered in our calculation. We have no certain proof of what revolution would entail. To have proof of what will happen in the future assumes that the future is but a replay, or sterile extension, of the past. The best we can envision are probabilities. Revolutionary thinking requires this best, if we are thinking about a just revolution in which "the damage likely to be incurred is not disproportionate to the injury suffered."

Means and Morality

This is a murky business. It's a long way from Frodo in the land of Mordor, where the forces of light are pitted against the legions of darkness. Those who have experienced anything of the sun in the Shire of Eriador know that revolution is made in the Mountains of Shadow. The path of revolution is still more perilous because it seeks not to destroy but to possess the Ring. Shades of Gollum. But come, you say, our story is not written by J. R. R. Tolkien but by Che, Fidel, Fanon, DeBray, and Shaull. Of course you are right. But one wonders who better tells it like it is.

If anyone thinks revolution means pot in Grant Park and skinny-dipping at public beaches, he should skip this section.

A just war is one that employs only legitimate and moral means. This seems absurdly anachronistic in the era of Hiroshima, Dresden, napalm, anti-missile missiles, and CBW. We are far from the medieval Truce of God and Peace of God in which it was assumed that men of honor could in times of war agree on moral restraints in battle. Learned tomes have been written detailing the decline of restraint in what we like to call our civilization. Our threshold of indignation is fast rising. There are so many atrocities to protest that the very word "atrocity" seems to lose its meaning. Is there any means left that is *inherently* evil, *deontologically* evil, so that the deed violates the very structure of creation? The Nuremberg Tribunal said there is. "Crimes against humanity" cannot be justified by any appeal to expediency or to the search for a greater good. Nuremberg suggested that, although we might not know what absolute good is, we do know absolute evil. But who then is to say what is a crime against humanity except in retrospect? And, as we know, history is written by the victors.

Guerrilla means, literally, a little war. Vietnam demonstrates that guerrilla warfare need not be diminutive. Certainly the moral problems in guerrilla warfare are at least as big and complex as in "real" warfare. A revolution, understood as a fundamental change by force in the social and political system, need not be carried out by means of guerrilla tactics. In the United States, for example, a revolution from the Right, conducted by the military in collusion with a substantial portion of the business and other establishments, might be relatively quick and bloodless. The scenario has been outlined in "Seven Days in May" and other films and books. It is not incredible.

The scenario for revolution from the Left is more complicated. The head of the Young People's Socialist League recently characterized as "absurd" and "fantastic" the notion current in some SDS and PLP circles that American revolutionary action can find guiding precedents in the revolutions of the Soviet Union and, more particularly, China and North Vietnam. Yet revolutionary theory does not emerge from nothing and it was therefore predictable that American revolutionaries are influenced by Marxist-Leninist-Maoist thought. With allowances for the peculiarities of the American situation, the three phases of the revolutionary struggle are:

Phase One. Propaganda, disruption, subversion. The oppressed masses are educated, there are strategic acts of terrorism designed for maximum psychological effect. Enlistment is based on real existing grievances against the regime and the social order.

Phase Two. Guerrilla warfare begins in earnest, with expanded acts of terror "calculated to shake confidence in the existing order." This includes a campaign to kill, kidnap, or otherwise intimidate any persons or institutions that give the appearance of being effectively concerned about the society's problems and might have some chance of limited success. Every appearance of reformism must be discredited. The *best* and the *worst*—that is, those who make reform credible and those who are most obviously corrupt—are brought before isolated communities and ceremoniously executed, sometimes with mutilation, and frequently with their families.

Part of the purpose of Phase Two is to drive the regime into taking severe countermeasures of repression and reprisal. As the regime attacks innocent people and becomes increasingly harsh it strengthens the revolution by intensifying popular resentment against itself. The regime can be counted on to fall into this trap.

Phase Three. As the regime is progressively defeated, demoralized, and desperate, the revolutionary forces invite more conventional combat. Finally, the regime and its allies lose heart, their will is broken, and the revolutionary war is crowned by success. The revolution, which has been able to capture the banners of nationalism and to present itself as the thrust of the future, then makes a temporary accommodation with its enemy. There follows a brief period of "reconciliation" during which the revolutionary force solidifies its absolute control.

The above is only a quick summary of the three-phase revolutionary theory, and in this form it tends to sound a bit slick, simplistic, and cynical. But it is plausible, as witness the last twenty years in Vietnam. No doubt were General Giap commanding operations from the corner of Fulton and Nostrand in the Bedford-Stuyvesant section of Brooklyn, extensive revisions would be in order. Nevertheless, the basic scenario is the model subscribed to by most revolutionaries here and in other parts of the world.

Some of the moral problems should be obvious. Of course, and as we have noted before, if one believes that the revolution is self-authenticating—as in the *Catechism of a Revolutionist*—there can be, by definition, no moral problems, for there are no outside points of reference by which the revolution can be criticized. This is not the belief that informs this discussion.

The revolution, it should be clear, is not an expanded teach-in or a more vigorous form of what we now call Community Organization. "Winning the hearts and minds of the people" is a deceptive phrase used by revolutionaries and the counterinsurgency alike. The revolutionaries' task, according to William O'Brien in *War and/or Survival*, is to "persuade the people by every means, fair or foul, that *they*, the revolutionaries, will be the future rulers of the society and that the incumbent regime, its supporters, and its collaborators are doomed." Whichever side is able to provide the greater security and general welfare will "win the hearts and minds of the people." This, I believe, is not an excessively cynical approach to the political consciousness of the masses. It should certainly be agreed to by those who insist most vehemently that the American masses have been brainwashed into accepting their role as instruments in a consumer society. Lenin and other revolutionary realists had no illusions about the revolution being, as it were, voted into power by popular mandate. On the contrary, a revolutionary situation exists, the revolutionary elite makes the most of it, and only afterward does the general populace acknowledge that the revolution was made in their behalf.

The revolutionary must learn to "think the unthinkable." The matter of torture illustrates this point as well as any. Revolutionary wars tend to skirt the niceties of international law. In Indochina and Algeria, the French acquired an expertise about counterinsurgency warfare that has resulted in a considerable literature about such matters as the uses, techniques and limitations of torture.

It is not hard to imagine that in the heat of revolutionary conflict the Deputy Inspector of the New York City police falls into the hands of the insurgents. He knows the details of an imminent plan aimed at eliminating a large part of the revolutionary leadership. He refuses to talk. Should torture be used? If so, what kind and how much is "moral and legitimate"? As much as necessary to make him talk? Let those who believe this situation utterly fanciful go back to revolutionary skinny-dipping.

William O'Brien, who has a penchant for contemplating unpleasantries, writes about the moral use of torture to obtain vital information:

> Torture can only, if ever, be justified as an official policy for which responsible commanders must answer.
> Second, the torturers must be trained to do their job with the least morally offensive means and in such a way as to do the least possible permanent physical and psychological damage to the victim. If they take advantage of their grim work to engage in gratuitous barbarism and sadism their moral guilt is manifest, and, to repeat, the legal, moral and military responsibility of their commanders is engaged.

O'Brien adds, in a somewhat caustic vein:

> It is reported that drafted seminarians in the French army in Algeria, when ordered to serve as interrogators, worked the "electros," which tortured through electric shocks, "gently." Will the priest-guerrillas of Latin America find "gentle" means of torturing their enemies to obtain the information which may be the difference between survival and annihilation by the counterinsurgents? Or will they take a walk and say some prayers while a tough leftist rebel does the job?

The grim aspects of armed revolution understandably make more attractive such alternatives as Gandhi's Satyagraha and the militant non-violence of Martin Luther King. In these strategies the axiom that "the means is the end in the process of becoming" is observed assiduously, the purpose being to redeem rather than destroy the enemy. Such struggle assumes that "the enemy" is also within all of us, that there is a fragility in the human condition, that the beast of violence, once released, will inevitably result in self-destruction. This assumption is intolerable to the armed revolutionary. In his view, this assumption is not one of modesty but of self-doubt that inhibits forthright action, it is an outrageous blurring of who is the oppressor and who is the liberator. It is inaccurate and unjust. The movement away from non-violence is usually attributed to impatience, which is a neutral, perhaps slightly negative, term in moral language. But the resort to violence is also seen, by many who advocate it, as a protest against the injustice of a non-violent rationale that seems to lump together good and bad in the idea of shared responsibility, in the idea that oppressor and oppressed are in some fundamental way the same. In impatience and in righteous indignation "revolutionary reality" is clarified in the deed of violence.

The revolutionary reality is not transformed into the revolutionary strategy simply by the deed of violence, however. Violence plus education, or propaganda, is only in the "first phase" of the revolutionary struggle. If it stops there, it is not revolution but violent reformism. Violent reformism, as we have seen, is what some advocate and practice today, although they mistakenly call it violent revolution. Revolution involves more than the willingness to brandish guns or firebomb an occasional slum building. One must have the stomach for selective terrorism. I have heard young people speak admiringly of Che's unwillingness to intimidate the Bolivian peasants in order to enlist them in his cause. As admirable as this may be, and whether one thinks of Che in terms of grand tragedy or farce, his unwillingness to use terrorism is probably part of the reason for the unquestioned disaster of the Bolivian campaign.

In the second phase armed revolution requires the elimination of liberal, counterrevolutionary elements. Useful alliances could be formed in the first phase, for the liberals and "liberal radicals" played an important role in interpreting the insurgency's purpose and giving it a degree of popular credibility. But now those who were once useful have become inimical to the revolution, not so much in their overt hostility as in their ability to persuade people that there is an alternative to armed revolution. The more radicalized liberals will welcome first phase violence as a useful prod for implementing their programs of reform. But when the revolution determines the beginning of the second phase, the revolution must take the initiative in terminating these alliances, making clear that the issue is joined and the only question is whether one is for or against the revolution. The "best" of the reformers must be ranked with the regime itself as enemies of the revolution. Second-phase armed revolution in the United States at present requires the effective elimination of persons such as Galbraith, McGovern, McCarthy, Randolph, Harrington, Goodwin, Chávez, and, if someone had not already seen to it, Martin Luther King.

The targeting of strategic terrorism is highly problematic. In one Latin American country the rebels' plan to gain support among the people by assassinating policemen backfired John Gerassi reports, "because every slain policeman in that society of very large families had so many relatives, all unable to see the death as a political act that might help them, able to see it only as a personal loss." The revolutionary may lament the lack of political consciousness among the relatives, but it is not surprising.

Two similar miscalculations in the United States are the effort of a handful of black revolutionaries to scapegoat the Jews and the anti-"pig" compaign of various white radicals. The first jeopardized the alliance with liberals which is still crucial, since not even the most passionate revolutionary in the United States, I hope, thinks we are in the second phase of the struggle. The undifferentiated thrust against police runs into the same problem encountered by the Latin Americans. This is particularly unfortunate because it is assumed by almost everyone that any effective revolutionary movement must include the blue-collar worker and poor white, the very community with traditional ties to police work. In these instances, the mo-

rality and the effectiveness of terrorism as means are inter-
twined.

Training for armed revolution requires a re-education
of some of the most fundamental human instincts around
which our notions of morality revolve. Consider, for example, the matter of friendship, of personal honor in human relations. In conventional war, as distinct from revolution, the dynamic of friendship is heightened and indeed
exploited. The tradition of the "buddy system" in combat,
the fact that friends and families are in most cases all
on the same side, combine to create a situation in which
one's loyalty to the cause is coterminous with his loyalties
as a private person. Fighting for America is the same thing
as keeping faith with relations and personal commitments.
One of the purposes, already in the first phase of the
struggle, is to divide loyalties, to bring commitments into
conflict.

We have seen many instances of this in connection with
soldiers refusing to serve in Vietnam. Another particularly
dramatic occasion was the refusal of black soldiers sta-
tioned in Texas to board a plane for Chicago where they
might have been ordered to act against relatives and
friends in connection with disturbances surrounding the
'68 convention. Most people, like these soldiers, are not
able to suspend personal loyalties in favor of political
cause. Not so the revolutionary.

The revolutionary views friendship as, at best, instrumental to the struggle. The influence of personal commitments must never be permitted to have priority over the
revolution. Conventional notions of honor are to be set
aside. The appeal to "conscience," so prominent now
among draft resisters and others, must be rigidly restricted.
The revolution, not conscience, is the guiding point of
reference for behavior. In questions of war and personal
loyalty, conscience must conform to revolutionary reality.
The idea that conscience is an autonomous court of appeal must be vigorously rejected as a bourgeois distortion.

Lenin particularly despised the pacifists and conscientious objectors who wanted a "premature" end of the First World War, thereby destroying the war's usefulness to the revolutionary struggle. "War is no accident and no 'sin' as the Christian reverends think . . . The strikes of the conscientious objectors and similar opposition to war are nothing but pitiful, cowardly, idle dreams. It is simply insane to talk about abolishing capitalism without a frightful civil war or without a succession of such wars."

The move "from resistance to revolution," a move which many young men see themselves as making, is not a natural progression or intensification. It is in many instances a complete reversal, at least in terms of its ethical judgment.

Deserters in Sweden and Canada talk about "politicizing" their act of desertion. That is, at first they may have left the military because they were repulsed by the evil of Vietnam and of American militarism. They could not, in conscience, kill or permit themselves to be killed in a fundamentally unjust cause. It was largely a matter of personal morality. "Now," one deserter told me, "I see my motivation was screwed up. I thought you just had to follow your conscience. But political analysis is more important than conscience. It worked out OK in this case because our [the deserters'] feeling turned out to be right about the war and everything . . . But now I might do a lot of things that are against what I used to call my conscience, if it would help the [desertion] movement."

The consensus of revolutionary morality that still prevails today is well expressed by Lenin: "Our morality, then, consists solely in close discipline and in conscious war against the exploiters. We do not believe in external principles of morality and we will expose this deception. [Revolutionary] morality is identical with the fight for strengthening the dictatorship of the proletariat." In the same connection, the revolutionary "must be prepared to make every sacrifice, and, if necessary, even resort to all sorts of cunning, schemes, and stratagems to employ illegal methods, to evade and conceal the truth, in order to penetrate [bourgeois] organizations, to remain in them, and conduct the Communist work in them at all cost."

At the University of Michigan it was explained to me by a young revolutionary that morality according to Mao is quite a different thing. The student, an enthusiastic reader of Herman Hesse and other such literary incense, asserted that the "community of the cadre" according to Mao is simply the revolutionary version of *Narcissus and Goldmund.* He added that we must look to Asia for our revolutionary thought today because "they don't have the kinds of moral hangups that we have in the West." That he was raised in the culture of Pittsburgh, U.S.A., seemed to him a matter of indifference. I did not argue with him, so desperate seemed his state of revolutionary euphoria.

Whether according to Mao or American provocateurs, the logic of revolutionary morality does not seem to have changed much from Lenin's statement, nor does it seem likely that it could. John Wilson, former deputy chairman of SNCC, writes in "Hard Talk on Organizing the Revolution" (*Renewal,* Feb. 1969) that we must move into bourgeois organizations "to destroy them through dissension and other means, the same way we have destroyed some of the leftist organizations by dissension and bickering and fighting within . . . We have to begin to infiltrate the institutions of this society to try to make them what we want them to be by destroying them and rebuilding them."

Carl Davidson of SDS makes an interesting use of "conscience" and Western moral criteria, writing in *New Left Notes* (November 13, 1967):

> The institutions our resistance has desanctified and delegitimized, as a result of our action against their oppression of others, have lost all authority and hence all respect. As such, they have only raw coercive power. Since they are without legitimacy in our eyes, they are without rights. Insofar as individuals, such as recruiters, continue to re-

main in association with those institutions, they run the
risk of being given the same treatment . . . We can assert
the Nuremberg decisions and other past criteria of war
crimes as the criteria by which we, in conscience, decide
whether or not an institution and individuals associated
with that institution have lost their legitimacy and their
rights.

When it is understood that human rights attach not to the
individual but to institutions or movements, that they are
dependent upon a "legitimacy" that is defined politically,
it becomes easier to accept the uses of torture and terrorism which are otherwise so odious. Against Mr. Davidson,
however, it must be noted that the whole point of Nuremberg was to repudiate this understanding of human rights.

When the revolution "re-educates" people to engage in,
or at least countenance, actions that outrage their basic
humane instincts, it faces the problem of itself remaining
humane in its struggle and success. Without drawing unpleasant parallels, the problem at this limited point is similar to that confronting the Green Berets who must later
return to civilian life and forget the skills of brutalization
they have acquired. How can the revolutionary be trained
to break personal trusts when called upon to do so and
still maintain the revolutionary trust that must be present
among partisans?

Not everyone is assigned the more atrocious tasks, of
course. Again without pushing the parallel, Nazi Germany
was sensitive to the danger of a general dehumanization
and brutalization of the military. Great care was taken in
selecting those who supervised the final solution of the
Jewish problem. Those who could not "discipline" their
emotions of compassion and outrage at Auschwitz, for
instance, were considerately assigned elsewhere. I suspect,
however, that even the revisionist interpreters of Nuremberg in *New Left Notes* would agree that responsibility for
atrocities is not limited to those who personally commit
them.

Precisely the opposite strategy is used in the revolution.

Not everyone is assigned the more odious jobs. This avoids general shock and perhaps alienation from the movement. But participation in "outrageous" deeds is also a means of solidifying the movement. It is one thing for a person to pledge verbally his life, liberty, and sacred honor to the cause. But the pledge is more sure if sealed by blood. This is in part a romantic hangover from the childhood business of a mutual blood smudge signifying "blood brotherhood." But it also has a very practical side to it. If the revolutionary recruit is implicated in an act that is viewed as a crime in the larger society and is subject to severe penalties, he has nowhere to go but to the fellowship of the revolution. This is particularly effective if the act involves taking life. Outside the revolution he then has the prospect of neither life nor liberty. And, perhaps most important, only in the revolution will his honor be viewed as sacred. Inside he is a comrade, outside a criminal. Eliot has each of Henry's knights dip his sword in Becket's blood. The deed is done, their solidarity sealed, they face the judgment of history and of God *together*. Such are the dynamics of unity, touched by romanticism but grounded in human insight, in movements noble and obscene.

We have talked of torture, terrorism and personal honor. There are other unavoidable dilemmas to be resolved. A moments reflection on, for example, the bombing of stores and restaurants crowded with men, women and children raises questions worthy of a thought beforehand. Examples could be multiplied, but the nature of the moral issue should be clear.

Freya Stark was quoted earlier: Revolution "should be a pleasant operation, and it is only because we have fallen into the habit of contemplating its grim side only that our attitude to revolution has come to be unfriendly." No doubt I am guilty in this section of having contemplated the grim side of revolution. I know there are those who believe the revolution in the United States will not require some of the more distasteful tactics of revolutionary struggle. After all, there was Fidel's relatively humane undermining of Havana from the hills, and even Lenin, for all his tough language, took over the Winter Palace with half-comic ease. But I do not see capturing New York City from the Catskills, and I vividly remember how the Pentagon rather handily withstood all our incantations and imprecations of October 1967. We know of the "Reign of Terror" that *followed* the French Revolution, of the purges in the Soviet Union and, although we do not like to talk about it, of the executions in the early years of the Castro regime. Further, if anyone believes that the situation in the United States is like that of Russia in 1900 or Cuba in 1952, he has an enviable talent for fantasy. It is no less of an achievement if, recognizing the unique factors in the United States, he believes armed revolution from the Left would be comparatively quick and bloodless. If I have looked at "the grim side" it is because armed revolution in the United States and most other places is a grim prospect. Would-be revolutionaries who refuse to contemplate this are deceiving themselves and others, or perhaps they are just making radical noises.

I affirm the right to armed revolution. This is not merely a theoretical affirmation; I believe there are situations in which the right can be morally exercised. I believe also that there is no conflict of arms in which moral sensibilities and restraints are not violated. Those who engage in and support such conflict must wrestle with the agonizing questions of what are "the limits of permissibility," if any. The guidelines are few and contradictory. This much is certain: talk about revolution is credible only when men stop speaking about revolution in general and address themselves to particular revolutions, including the "moral means" by which they are pursued.

All of this is academic unless there is a reasonable hope for success. That is the next and final measure of a just revolution.

Will the Revolution Succeed?

Success seems a strange measurement of justice. Surely we reject the notion that "might makes right," whether it is the might of imperialist America or of a bellicose Chinese cadre member asserting that justice issues from the barrel of a gun. Success cannot make an unjust cause just. In certain circumstances, however, failure can make an otherwise just cause unjust. To put it more precisely, every condition of a just revolution might be met, clearly constituting the *right* to revolution, but if there is not "reasonable hope for success" it would be unjust to *exercise* that right.

The Vietnam war suggests a useful parallel. A few Christian ethicists have in recent years employed the "just war theory" to argue for the morality of the U.S. course in Vietnam. They claimed, wrongly, I am confident, that what this country was doing in Vietnam met the criteria of a just war. (This claim, incidentally, demonstrates more clearly than anything I have written the limitations of set formulas or principles in determining questions of justice.) Now, however, it is becoming apparent to these ethicists that the U.S. government did not have the determination to follow through on its commitment in Vietnam, chiefly because the government had not counted in advance on the anti-war political pressures on the home front. In short, they are saying, a war that is just on other counts may be unjust because the political weakness of the U.S. government precluded "reasonable hope for success." The cost of the war could be justified only by its successful conclusion. Although its premises are wrong this argument is instructive in its consistency.

The SDS slogan in the fall of 1969 is no longer "Bring the Boys Home" but "Bring the War Home." Before bringing the war home, in the full sense of armed revolution, we should calculate the chances of success. The call to calculate in advance will be denigrated by some as a strategy of delay, aimed at creating excessive inhibitions to revolutionary action. If asking about the justice of the revolution is inhibiting, there is some truth in the charge. But inhibiting action is not the purpose of this reflection. The purpose, quite simply, is to prevent, as much as possible, the doing of murder; murder being the alternative to justice.

The best revolutionary theory is future-oriented. Only the future reveals the meaning of the past, only in retrospect do we see what really happened. The future either repudiates or vindicates the decisions we make in the present. Only the success of the revolution can vindicate the will-to-revolution. Yet we do not know the future, we know only the present, and even that in small part. Through Reason we apprehend what are the possibilities and probabilities of the future. Our apprehension is often little more than intuitive and is always marked by high risk.

Conservative "rationality" de-emphasizes the possibility of the genuinely New in the future, assuming that things must continue as they have been. The radical consciousness, on the other hand, often fails to recognize the unity of reality, expecting a future totally discontinuous with the present. A future that annihilates the present also invalidates the revolutionary insights of the past and present. Thus the statement of a totally discontinuous future is, in the most precise sense, non-sense. To act on such a statement is a form of madness.

We can "know" some things about the very immediate future, less about the distant future. The radical mind is influenced by the memory of how often small events have had momentous and unexpected consequences. The radical is not intimidated by conventional cost-benefit accounting. He knows that many, and sometimes apparently "counter-productive," tactics must be tried in order to find something that "works." The true radical is trained in deeds of daring and courage, even when such deeds are viewed by others as derring-do and bravado.

Daring deeds take on a different coloration, however, when they involve the lives (I do not say property) of others. The issue changes from one of courage to one of right. Rennie Davis, one of the demonstration leaders in Chicago in 1968, was urged by some to call for a forceful takeover of the city. A moment's thought about what such a forceful takeover implies, including certain death for many, demonstrates that Davis was right in dismissing the suggestion out of hand. Similarly, if the Mobilization-sponsored "Death March" in Washington, D.C., in November 1969 were aimed at taking over the Capitol, it would be rightly condemned as a futile gesture. Such ideas would be in flagrant violation of revolutionary Reason. Leaders do not have the *right* to call for a suicidal bloodbath in which there is no "reasonable hope for success." However just the cause, such a call remains unjust.

In the revolution there is no substitute for success. It is different with the army of the established regime. In conventional war, hostilities can end and a truce can be signed on the basis of compromise. Because its purpose is to initiate a genuinely new order and to replace the regime, the revolution cannot compromise. As long as it remains with milder actions of the first phase, the revolution has an ambiguous existence. It can present itself as a movement of violent reformism and, if things do not work out, it need not go further. But once it crosses the line into the second phase, either in action or public intent, there is no turning back for the revolutionary.

The movement has gone too far. If it fails, the brothers may hope for clemency from the regime, but that is all. And even that is unlikely, since overt revolutionary action will accelerate the ascendency of the Right in ruling circles. The mere fact of serious revolutionary action discredits the liberals who were arguing all along that the insurgency is simply a healthy, if somewhat disruptive, restlessness for social change. If the liberals are not discredited by the falseness of their predictions, the revolution in the second phase must, as we have seen, neutralize them by terrorism. Needless to say, the courts would be of no use to the revolutionaries, for, under the influence of the Right, they would be thoroughly politicized. In the revolution, there is no substitute for success.

The success of the revolution does not here mean the achievement of all its revolutionary goals. Fifty years later, the Soviet Union admits it has traveled only a short way on the road to socialization. Most revolutions have a morning-after period of intense disappointment, which explains why revolutionary regimes resort to the notion of "permanent revolution," exhorting the people years after the supposed "victory" that the struggle has just begun. Forty years after the revolution in Mexico, the regime is called The Institutional Revolutionary Party. "We are beginning to see the first fruits of our revolutionary labor," Fidel tells a cheering Havana crowd in late 1969. The "success" at issue in this section can be limited simply to the revolution's taking over power, when the old regime is replaced by the revolutionary regime and the revolutionary leadership is in control.

"Success" in terms of achieving the revolutionary goals in the society is a much bigger subject. When John Wilson says we must move into "the institutions of this society to try to make them what we want them to be by destroying them and rebuilding them," it must be assumed that we know "what we want them to be" and that the achievement of that purpose will constitute the real "success" of the revolution.

The more limited success of installing the revolutionary regime requires that we engage in a revolutionary version of war games. In *The Urban Guerrilla*, Martin Oppenheimer does precisely that. He furnishes two scenarios of projected revolutionary uprisings of urban blacks and demonstrates that in the present circumstances such rebellions have no chance of success. Those who are today set on revolution, however, are building a black-white revolutionary alliance. Repression and counterinsurgency will not be the relatively simple matter of isolating black communities. Counterinsurgency will impinge upon, will discomfort, the whites as well. It is expected that this will increase resentment against the government on the part of whites. In places like Wilmington, Delaware, where, in the name of emergency, police-state measures were imposed in the black community for many months, it did not impinge on whites, except perhaps on the conscience of a sensitive few. If in future counterinsurgency actions the white community were discomforted, the question arises about whom the whites would blame. In present circumstances at least, it is almost inevitable that such discomfort would intensify resentment against the revolution rather than against the regime. The situation in Chicago in 1968 is not entirely parallel, of course, but the reported 80 per cent of Chicagoans who approved of the police riot is a relevant statistic.

Revolutionary war games should try to anticipate the likelihood of sympathetic uprisings within the military, civil service, labor unions, intelligentsia, and—increasingly important—the mass-media industry. The key to such scenarios is the fact that the vast majority of people have a greater passion for security than for adventure. Therefore, the question of "order" becomes central. Even those who may care deeply about justice will insist that there might be order without justice but there can be no justice without order. The success of the revolution depends upon convincing the politically effective portion of the population that there is a better chance for social order under the revolutionary leadership than under the old regime. Facing the abyss of disorder, the Americans for Democratic Action and the Minutemen can readily find grounds for agreement and common action.

Millions of dollars are being spent by police departments

for "riot control," that is counterinsurgency, weaponry. The National Guard is being strengthened on every front. Pentagon militarists assure us that after Vietnam it will still be necessary to maintain a standing force of more than two million for "other peace-keeping activities." Mr. John Mitchell and his cohorts in the Department of Republican Justice will not be discouraged in their hopes to obtain such useful counterinsurgency legal tools as "preventive detention." All these and other elements must enter into the calculus of revolution.

A just revolution is one in which there is reasonable hope for success. Anyone who calls for revolution but has not tried to think through the scenarios of its success and failure is not daring but self-indulgent. The times are too serious for posturing. Advocating revolution is not a matter of balls but of vision. To the degree that a person consciously contributes to an unjust revolution, he is guilty of its consequences. He earns the disdain of radical, liberal, and conservative alike. Above all, he earns the disdain of those true rebels who, in the courage of their uncertainties, have weighed the cost and surrender themselves to the exercise of that elementary political right, the right to revolution.

Conclusion

Who cares about the ethics of armed revolution? Certainly not the absolute pacifists whose commitment to militant non-violence is as clear as it is honorable. Certainly not those who despair of politics as an instrument of humanization; they seek their new order in communes and encounters where the only reality that matters is personal. Certainly not the Crazies for whom orderly thought is a betrayal of their bizarre authenticity, and who don't read books in any case. Certainly not conventional liberals who, as they unfailingly assure us, are too busy with their pragmatic problem-solving to worry about revolution. Certainly not the more radicalized liberals who condescendingly interpret today's call to revolution as the healthy sound of children protesting the mess their parents have made of things. Certainly not the public spokesmen for revolution who cannot be distracted from their rounds on the television talk-show circuit.

Who, then, is left to care about the ethics of revolution? Conservatives and reactionaries on the Right care. Some of the criticisms of the Movement expressed here are useful in bolstering their polemic against the Left. The grim questions intended as guidelines for thinking through the revolutionary prospect can be used to inhibit and even paralyze the thought and action of some radicals. But the questions must be posed, and we cannot prevent whatever use the Right may make of that.

The serious builders of a revolutionary movement care, at least those who have not succumbed to the fanaticism of a "revolutionary morality" that is self-authenticating and beyond questioning do. There are such people in the Black Panther Party, and at least a few in SDS and Progressive Labor circles, and still more in what is too disparagingly termed the Old Left. For them revolutionary verbiage has lost its potency to charm or shock, they have played all the variations of more-radical-than-thou and have outgrown the game. Now their attention is turned to the problems and possibilities, the rights and the wrongs, of making revolution. I hope this essay adds something to that reflection.

But this essay is chiefly intended for another audience. They are met on almost any college campus, in demonstrations and rallies, and in the boardrooms of the most prestigious cause organizations in the country. Some of them are only a few months or a few years old, politically speaking. Others are veterans of battles and jails in campaigns dating from the 1920s, they marched under the banners of Debs, Thomas, King, and Dellinger; their biographies are the story of modern radicalism in America. Still others are yesterday's liberals who have lost their faith in inevitable progress. And the blacks for whom the American promise seems ever elusive, always just beyond the government's next major program, waiting to be possessed on the other side of each new beginning in an endless succession of new beginnings. It is a tantalizing, teasing, mocking promise, nurtured by official statistics showing the black man getting a bigger piece of the action. Until the black man awakes to discover the promise has become a threat. It was not for this, this American Way of Life, that my forefathers yearned when, through interminable years of slavery, bloodshed and degradation, they sang of a New Day, a New Jerusalem, the Beloved Community.

"He who laughs has not yet received the terrible news," wrote Bertolt Brecht. This essay is intended for those who have stopped laughing. In whose minds there has formed the awesome thought of revolution. They are part of the Movement, yet individuals. Somewhere they heard that a man could gain the whole world and lose his own soul, and then he has gained nothing. They have seen the lust for power and recognized her as the bitch goddess that she is. Their political conscience has been refined in the fires of Auschwitz, Vietnam, and two hundred Newarks. In the dock at Nuremberg they recognize men not entirely unlike themselves. They sort through the shattered remnants of other movements and other dreams, and wonder about the limitations of politics in building the New Order for which good men hope.

Such men know there will be other Nurembergs, that there is within history a Reckoning, that, to some thing or some One, man is accountable. He stands under judgment.

I have written for such men as are prepared to consider a just revolution legitimately declared and in response to real injury, as a last resort and prosecuted with good intention, in which the damage incurred is not greater than the injury suffered, employing moral means and with a reasonable hope for success.

A WAGER

PETER L. BERGER
AND RICHARD JOHN NEUHAUS

The points on which we differ should be clear to the careful reader. The point at which we come together is a wager. The reader may want to join us on this course of calculated risk.

We agree that, whether or not an armed revolution is necessary, the United States is not ripe for it (we speak here only of the United States). We differ on the probabilities of such a necessity coming about. Both of us can conceive of a situation developing in America in which the criteria for a just revolution discussed in Neuhaus' essay (with which Berger, with some reservations, essentially agrees) would apply. Obviously Neuhaus can conceive of this more readily than Berger. It is equally obvious that only the future will reveal who is closer to the truth. Therein lies the wager.

We cannot afford to wait passively for the future to reveal itself. The question is what we do now. We agree that justice demands far-reaching changes in American life, particularly in the way American power is exercised in the world and at home. Both essays suggest the direction of this change. For both of us change must be informed by the lessons of Vietnam and of the racial crisis. Will such change come about short of revolution? In other words, are Vietnam and the racial crisis necessary consequences or avoidable distortions of the structure of American life? Berger says yes to the first question, believing that our present problems are not endemic to "the System."

Neuhaus is less sanguine about this and therefore more willing to consider the revolutionary alternative.

Revolution would make itself necessary when all reasonable efforts to achieve the changes demanded by justice are finally defeated. Berger says flatly that this has not happened. Neuhaus argues this is not yet clear. It will only become clear as we intensively press such efforts. And this we, conservative and radical alike, can do together. *One presses in the confidence that these efforts will confirm his belief in the reformability of American society. The other engages in the same efforts, confident that frustrated reformism will strengthen the revolutionary struggle that will then be necessary, but open to the possibility, however improbable, that successful reform will preclude the necessity of revolution.* For both, achieving a more just society without the enormous suffering of revolutionary struggle is the preferred outcome. For both, there is an agenda of urgent actions which alone can force the verdict of the future.